Praise for M. L. Buchman

One of our favorite authors.

RT Book Reviews

Buchman has catapulted his way to the top tier of my favorite authors.

Fresh Fiction

A favorite author of mine. I'll read anything that carries his name, no questions asked. Meet your new favorite author!

The Sassy Bookster, Flash of Fire

M.L. Buchman is guaranteed to get me lost in a good story.

The Reading Cafe, Way of the Warrior: NSDQ

I love Buchman's writing. His vivid descriptions bring everything to life in an unforgettable way.

Pure Jonel, Hot Point

NARRATE AND RECORD YOUR OWN AUDIOBOOK

a simplified guide

M. L. BUCHMAN

Buchman Bookworks

Copyright 2019 Matthew Lieber Buchman

Published by Buchman Bookworks, Inc.

All rights reserved.

This book, or parts thereof, may not be reproduced in any form without permission from the author.

Receive a free book and discover more by this author at: www.mlbuchman.com

Cover images:

Training © kbuntu | Depositphotos

Studio Microphone © summers | Depositphotos

All screen shots were made using Adobe Audition CC running on Windows 10 (current to 7/2019). The principles are unlikely to change but the dialog boxes may.

Sign up for M. L. Buchman's
newsletter today

and receive:
Release News
Free Short Stories
a Free book

Get your free book today. Do it now.
free-book.mlbuchman.com

Other works by M. L. Buchman: *(* - also in audio)*

Thrillers

Dead Chef
Swap Out!
One Chef!
Two Chef!

Miranda Chase
Drone*
Thunderbolt*

Romantic Suspense

Delta Force
Target Engaged*
Heart Strike*
Wild Justice*
Midnight Trust*

Firehawks
MAIN FLIGHT
Pure Heat
Full Blaze
Hot Point*
Flash of Fire*
Wild Fire
SMOKEJUMPERS
Wildfire at Dawn*
Wildfire at Larch Creek*
Wildfire on the Skagit*

The Night Stalkers
MAIN FLIGHT
The Night Is Mine
I Own the Dawn
Wait Until Dark
Take Over at Midnight
Light Up the Night
Bring On the Dusk
By Break of Day
AND THE NAVY
Christmas at Steel Beach
Christmas at Peleliu Cove

WHITE HOUSE HOLIDAY
Daniel's Christmas*
Frank's Independence Day*
Peter's Christmas*
Zachary's Christmas*
Roy's Independence Day*
Damien's Christmas*

5E
Target of the Heart
Target Lock on Love
Target of Mine
Target of One's Own

Shadow Force: Psi
At the Slightest Sound*
At the Quietest Word*

White House Protection Force
Off the Leash*
On Your Mark*
In the Weeds*

Contemporary Romance

Eagle Cove
Return to Eagle Cove
Recipe for Eagle Cove
Longing for Eagle Cove
Keepsake for Eagle Cove

Henderson's Ranch
Nathan's Big Sky*
Big Sky, Loyal Heart*
Big Sky Dog Whisperer*

Love Abroad
Heart of the Cotswolds: England
Path of Love: Cinque Terre, Italy

Other works by M. L. Buchman:

Contemporary Romance (cont)

Where Dreams
Where Dreams are Born
Where Dreams Reside
Where Dreams Are of Christmas
Where Dreams Unfold
Where Dreams Are Written

Science Fiction / Fantasy

Deities Anonymous
Cookbook from Hell: Reheated
Saviors 101

Single Titles
The Nara Reaction
Monk's Maze
the Me and Elsie Chronicles

Non-Fiction

Strategies for Success
Managing Your Inner Artist/Writer
Estate Planning for Authors*
Character Voice
Narrate and Record Your Own Audiobook*

Short Story Series by M. L. Buchman:

Romantic Suspense

Delta Force
Delta Force

Firehawks
The Firehawks Lookouts
The Firehawks Hotshots
The Firebirds

The Night Stalkers
The Night Stalkers
The Night Stalkers 5E
The Night Stalkers CSAR
The Night Stalkers Wedding Stories

US Coast Guard
US Coast Guard

White House Protection Force
White House Protection Force

Contemporary Romance

Eagle Cove
Eagle Cove

Henderson's Ranch
Henderson's Ranch

Where Dreams
Where Dreams

Thrillers

Dead Chef
Dead Chef

Science Fiction / Fantasy

Deities Anonymous
Deities Anonymous

Other
The Future Night Stalkers
Single Titles

Contents

About This Book	xi
Introduction	xiii
1. The Basics	1
2. Your Narrator Voice	7
3. Character Voices	17
4. The Recording Space	29
5. Equipment	39
6. A Recording Session	53
7. Intro to Engineering	67
8. Engineering	77
9. The Listen	97
10. Final Steps	105
Afterword	113
About the Author	115
Also by M. L. Buchman	117

About This Book

Audio is the up-and-coming market, but the price of entry can be a horrific $300-500 per finished hour and up.

M. L. Buchman has recorded and published over 30 audio titles —himself.

Here he covers the basics you need to record your own audiobooks.

- *How to decide if it's the best option.*
- *When you should outsource the engineering.*
- *Why you're wrong when you "hate your own voice."*
- *Tools, techniques, and free studio space ideas.*
- *A step-by-step guide to recording and engineering your own audiobook.*
- *How to quantify direct, and most importantly of all, indirect costs.*

This simplified guide delivers the confidence to tackle the unique opportunity of "Read by Author."

Introduction

So, you think you want to tackle recording your own audiobook.

Fantastic!

It is fun and potentially lucrative. It can also be frustrating, expensive in unexpected ways, and may not pay out.

This book was written to help you maximize the fun and profit and minimize all the other crap.

Why this book

There are dozens of ways to record a book and hundreds, literally, of possible settings to engineer your audiobook.

This volume is intended to cut through all of the choices and lay out a single clear path that has worked for this author in narrating over thirty of his own titles. Are there better techniques? I like to think not. Are there other, equally good techniques? Absolutely.

This is neither a technical treatise on audio recording nor an education in sound engineering. It is about the straightforward steps necessary to record a quality audiobook for public sale.

Why me

I spent over seven years as a live theater sound operator (among other roles). My mentors were two of the leading audio engineers in the Pacific Northwest. They were involved in everything from small productions that would eventually give birth to Seattle's Fringe Theater movement to touring with major Seattle bands. They engineered recordings for the Seattle Symphony and live broadcasts of Seattle Opera performances.

While I was never a truly brilliant sound man in the way that they were, I received a deep education that would stand me in good stead when I produced my first audiobooks starting in 2013.

About this book

This book is intended to serve two purposes:

1. Help make the decision about the whether or not recording your own audiobook is the right choice for you. (Chapter 1)
2. A simplified guide to the exact steps to doing so. (The rest of the book)

In the course of the simplified guide we'll discuss:
Basic and advanced techniques of giving your characters a voice.
Dos and Don'ts of audio narration.
Choosing software, computers, and a microphone.
Selecting a good recording space / booth.

Introduction

How to record.

A simple guide on how to approach the complex task of engineering—or whether this step is best outsourced.

The crucial "The Listen" step.

Properly saving your files.

A few tips on markets and marketing.

A Few Essentials

Nonfiction Narration

While this book primarily discusses fiction narration, almost every single technique is equally applicable to nonfiction. Where there are differences, I'll try to point them out.

Per Finished Hour

This is an essential concept in audiobooks; everything is based on the cost per completed hour of narrated audio. Depending on your skill and that of the engineer (which may also be you), the process can vary from three to ten hours of work to create one finished hour of audio. An audiobook is best narrated at about 9,000 words per hour. So, a 45,000 word book will be approximately 5 finished hours.

Let's plunge in.

1

The Basics

A Little Vocabulary

THERE ARE three major aspects to creating an audiobook:

Recording – Like writing is placing the words on the written page, it is actually as simple a concept as it appears: recording the sound of your, the narrator's, voice. In many ways this is also the easiest step of creating an audiobook. The words are already written. The characters are already complete in almost every respect except for the sound of their narrated voice. However, there is also a great deal of technique to be learned and, just like writing, the fun and challenge of learning never ends.

Engineering – This is a two-stage process of mechanical cleanup of a file and proofing the recording for technical and recording errors. This is far and away the most complex and time-consuming part of the process. In fact, we'll break it into another three parts: 1) Processing, 2) "The Listen," and 3) Corrections.

Marketing – Because of the rapidly changing dynamics of the marketplace (especially at the time of this writing), we'll touch on this only briefly and in the most general of ways.

Five Ways to Make an Audiobook

There are presently five primary ways to produce an audiobook. Each has its own advantages and disadvantages. As you read the list below, consider how you feel about each of these factors and how they might affect your decision of what the best course might be for you.

Of these five options, this book only addresses the first two.

Record your own and engineer your own

Costs: Minimal (as little as $300 to set up plus $30/month at this time).

Effort: Time cost is highest (as high as 10 hours per finished hour until you get rolling). This book contains a number of techniques to reduce that to 3–5 hours per finished hour.

Control: 100% yours.

Profits: 100% yours.

Record your own and hire out the engineering (this will be the best fit for most home narrators).

- Costs: Minimal (as little as $300) plus $50–$125 per finished hour for engineering.
- Effort: Time cost is moderate to low (2–5 hours per finished hour).
- Control: Control of recording, not of engineering.

- Profits: 100% to you.

Royalty Share programs (such as currently offered by ACX).

Costs: $0.

Effort: Time required is typically 2–3 hours per finished hour.

Control: You can accept or reject the narrator and request fixes.

Profits: 50% to you, 50% to narrator.

Pay for the narrator yourself.

- Costs: Cost $150–$500+ per finished hour.
- Effort: Time required is approximately 2–3 hours per finished hour.
- Control: You can accept or reject the narrator and request fixes.
- Profits: 100% to you. First it pays off the narrator investment, but then, if it is a sudden success, you own the recording and it continues to pay 100% to you.

License the audio rights to a professional audio publisher.

- Costs: $0.
- Effort: Time required is approximately 1.5 hours per finished hour. (If the publisher even

offers you a chance to perform a proofing listen to suggest changes and identify an problems. Mine didn't.)
- Control: Little to none.
- Profits: 8%–12% typical. May not earn out the advance, assuming you got one. If it takes off, you'll make significantly less money.

Technical Quality

There is a reason I didn't list technical quality above. I listened to my first audiobooks in the 1980s sitting on my couch in front of my stereo system (it was major because I was a sound geek from when I built my first amplifier back in junior high). I spent hours sitting in the ideal position, appreciating the story and the quality of the recording. When they advanced from cassettes to CDs (as early as 1984), I advanced with them whenever my budget allowed.

A professional publisher and the most expensive narrators will have truly exceptional studios and microphones. Most narrators, especially in the royalty share category, will probably be using equipment little better than you would.

The key here is that today's listener is in the car, out for a jog, or looking for a distraction over $15 earbuds. Any decent quality, error-free recording will be greatly enjoyed by the listener.

Are there a few people who will be disappointed by a lack of technical quality while using their $400 studio-quality headphones? Probably not. The affordable tools today are simply so good that they will enjoy it as well.

Some authors choose to record their own audiobook because they're control freaks (a category this author absolutely belongs to). They spent all the effort to get the words on the page just right and now they want to make sure that hard work is honored in audio.

Other authors start recording their own books for simple economic reasons—they can't afford to pay a narrator, at least not early in their career. In the process of building their skills, they also discover how much fun it can be.

Some wish to maximize their back end profits by ensuring 100% ownership but are unwilling or unable to afford a professional narrator.

Alternatively, I have a friend who came out of radio broadcasting way back. She won't record her own audiobooks because it would be a total rabbit hole for her—she *loves* the recording and engineering process and fears that it would consume all of her writing time.

Knowing your reasons will help you plug this kind of information into your business plan and manage your ongoing efforts. Personally, I could easily lose myself in nothing but recording all of my back titles, but I know that would frustrate my audience awaiting new stories and so I strive to strike a balance. For me as a full-time writer? I aim to spend between six and eight hours per week on recording and marketing audio. I give the engineering tasks that creates, of an additional 15–20 hours, to my assistant.

Abridged vs. Unabridged

Abridged versions were created to keep costs down back when every 60–90 minutes cost an additional cassette tape or audio CD. Now we're in the age of downloadable MP3s and these cost factors are no longer an issue.

As a listener, I hate abridged versions. I'm not interested in a "Story in a hurry." I want the full experience as the author intended.

As a writer, an abridgment—especially a good one—is a difficult and time-consuming task to create. And they're also less popular. I've spoken with a number of librarians (folks who track the listening habits of a *lot* of patrons) and they've simply stopped ordering abridged audiobooks because of their significantly lower popularity.

Don't shortchange your fans, give them the whole thing.

2

Your Narrator Voice

LET'S discuss three illustrative tales about a narrator's voice before we talk about how to create your *own* narrator's voice.

Stephen King

If ever there was an author who should *not* read their own books, it's Stephen King. Bear with me for a moment on this. Better yet, go and listen to one of the audiobooks that he recorded. (Not *On Writing*, but rather a piece of fiction such as the *Dark Tower* series or watch an online video of him reading to a public forum.)

He *reads* his book aloud. No characterization. Little emotion—almost monotone. He simply reads it.

However, I will take a book read by Stephen King over many others, even though horror is not one of my preferred genres.

Why?

Because Stephen King is the absolute master of the written word. He and I write in the same language,

English, and we use the same fourteen punctuation marks. (Twelve really, because how often do you see [square brackets] and {braces} in fiction?)

With the addition of the intelligent use of paragraph, scene, and chapter breaks, he can control your heartrate—even whether or not you're breathing.

And in listening to him "read" one of his audiobooks, I get to experience every nuance of how he intended it to be. I'm going to repeat that: *of how **HE** intended it to be.*

There is little drama in his narrations, but there is immense impact. That is the true power of "read by author" recordings.

The Southern Belle

One of my traditionally published titles was sold by my publisher into an audio format. Per our contract, they submitted three narrator samples to me. Along with the samples, they said, "Please pick this one." I didn't get to pick, only to recommend, but I appreciated their phrasing.

I listened to all three carefully.

Now I need to preface something here: the book was military romantic suspense. There are a number of scenes that take place aboard a military helicopter in the heat of the action.

The audition piece was a three-minute segment of the crew discussing relationships over the intercom in the midst of a battle sequence—a real challenge for any narrator. As the three samples were all done by professional narrators, they all crossed over that bar easily.

But the one the publisher wanted me to pick had just the sweetest Southern voice. Imagine a hot and heavy battle aboard an "MH-60 DAP Hawk helicopter" being read in Antebellum Sothern Belle English. I just couldn't wrap my head around it.

I pointed this out to the publisher, who sighed that I was probably right, and they chose another narrator—one who did a masterful job.

There are some voices that just don't match the material...I think. I've second-guessed my recommendation numerous times over the years because the narrator they turned down was the great Johanna Parker, the narrator of Charlene Harris' Sookie Stackhouse novels! Audiobook listeners often follow narrators. Did my advice turn away, or rather never engage with, an extra thousand or ten thousand fans? Or did it spare a thousand unhappy listeners expecting a different experience? I'll never know.

I've listened to some of her recordings since. Several of her different characterizations would have been a much better fit for my books than the tone of the languid South that was in the audition. With what I know now, I might have pushed back for a re-audition asking for a less accented and more sharply paced reading. But I didn't.

The Production Geek

Creating audio definitely takes time. And there was a period of a couple years during the initial launch of my indie writing career when I simply couldn't make time to record audio. So, I auditioned various narrators.

One in particular stands out as a good example. I told him that I just wanted my book read. Not Stephen-King-style read, but not some overly-dramatic exposition either. Nothing fancy, no music, just a good dramatic reading.

He sent me back two samples.

The "basic" version, he read very dramatically. He dubbed in some music and drastically altered the voice electronically to simulate dialog over a radio from another helicopter.

He also created a "real" version of how he felt it should be produced. He and his wife read the male and female parts. There was music, sound effects for gunfire and helicopters, and so much drama it was difficult to find the words. He was passionate in his arguments favoring this version—he loves what he does.

However, we had such different visions of what an audiobook should be that we couldn't come to terms sufficient to move ahead with the collaboration.

He's a successful narrator and his finished product is always a fun and wild ride, but it is a production in and of itself. I'm a control-freak writer, I just want it to be about my words.

Summary

You must decide what *you* want to present for *your* listeners as an audiobook experience. That's worth repeating: We need to ask what we think would be best for our *listeners*.

Do we want:

- The read-by-author experience of Stephen King no matter what the shortcomings.
- The voice to be truly appropriate for the book, all other considerations aside.
- A solo reading.
- A two-person or full-cast reading of multiple voices.
- A full production dramatic version.

Music in Audiobooks

Music was originally introduced into audiobooks as a cue to the listener to flip over their audio cassette. Every side ended with music and the next side continued with the same music underneath the words to ease the transition. The last line of one side was also typically repeated as the first line of the next.

Some consider this as a requirement of audiobooks. It isn't. Now, in the age of electronically delivered audio, it's an aesthetic choice—one that you'll have to make about your own audiobooks. (Do make sure to get a copyright license for any music you do use.)

My proofreader (who is awesome) tells me that the tradition traces back even further onto records. She partly learned to read from her *Alice in Wonderland* recording, which came with a read-along book. The Mad Hatter giggled each time the listener / reader was supposed to turn the page.

Studying Voice

Audiobook Narrators

The first method, obviously, is listening to audiobooks. But remember, you're now studying to be a narrator yourself. Listen twice, at least, to any audiobook you particularly enjoy.

The first listen is to enjoy the story.

The second and successive listens are to study the narrator. Even better, listen with a copy of the book in your lap (after the first time). Add a notepad to scribble down what you learned.

For now, study the narrator, we'll get into their characterization and other techniques in the next section. Start learning to hear the narrator separate from the story.

Tip: Each time you find yourself listening to the story rather than the narrator, stop and force yourself to return to the last point you recall listening to the narrator.

- How dramatic is the reading?
- How distinguishable are the various character voices?
- Is it a flat "King-ish" reading or is it rife with "Production Geek"?
- Is the voice appropriate for the story or do you wish it had been told differently? Perhaps with the same narrator but read differently.
- And my favorite question: Do I enjoy this particular narration? There are some narrators I really do, and some I really don't. Ask yourself why you feel that way.

If you have a favorite narrator(s), try one of their books in a drastically different genre. What did they do differently in a romance, a thriller, science fiction, or mystery?

Do you write nonfiction? It is an incredibly popular area of audiobooks. Listen and ask yourself what they do to *not* bore you to tears with their production. Also, how do they handle pictures, charts, illustrations, and graphs.

I consider listening to other audiobook narrators as the most technical aspect of studying narration and we'll definitely revisit it more.

. . .

STORYTELLERS

Storytellers are a fascinating contrast. Almost always a single person, their entire strategy is to engage the listener with their voice. A good storyteller can captivate and engage their audience for minutes or even hours with no other tools than voice and a few gestures (and a good tale). Many will tend toward a more dramatic telling, but any future narrator will learn any number of useful tactics from them.

Personally, I think that one of the most ignored teachings is the dramatic pause. Yes, a storyteller can combine it with a sly smile and a slow inspection of the audience. But too many audiobooks are relentlessly paced as the narrator thinks it is only about the words and less about a story well told.

If finding a storyteller seems too unlikely, simply do an online search. Folk fairs, weekend farmer's markets, or a weeknight event at a local pub are just a few of the locations to find storytellers.

For a time, I was a member of Toastmasters, a group dedicated to teaching you how to speak in public. Go online and listen to the finalists in their national competitions. These are brilliant speakers—among the best in the world. Their final presentations are, by design, very brief. But they are frequently telling humorous or touching tales in a thoroughly engaging way.

PLAYS AND OTHER MEDIA

Perhaps not musicals, for obvious reasons, but dramatic plays are another place to study voice. Actors, with little more window dressing than an unmoving stage set behind them, must captivate you with their voice. (For writers, this is also a great place to study dialog if that is a weak spot for you.)

Television and film are rarely good tools for studying narration. These highly visual mediums use techniques unavailable to the audiobook narrator. Will they be useful in the future? I've already seen several examples of where a book is redone as a dramatic audio-visual production downloadable to your phone, television, computer, or whatever. They have a long way to go, but there is work being done in this area.

Narration Lessons

This is certainly an option, but a modicum of care is needed in choosing your class.

Acting classes focus on stage and screen techniques. Some of that focus is on vocalization and characterization, but much of it is also focused on motion, interaction with other actors, and the myriad aspects of advanced stagecraft.

Voice lessons typically imply singing.

Toastmasters will hone your short-tale structure skills as much as your voice and can be a very good option.

Joining a storytelling group sounds like great fun, though I've never done this.

As you advance, there are some professional narrators who provide coaching. The secret here is to not engage in coaching that is too advanced for where your skillset currently lies.

My best advice engages a simple concept: *you already know what your characters sound like.* So, the best option is to go into the audio recording booth and:

Give yourself permission to sound stupid.

I'm serious!

By being willing to try dramatic tones, pauses, and many other techniques, we will rapidly learn what we as author / narrators like and don't like in a recording. If you don't push boundaries, especially at first, how will you find where you want your voice to land?

We'll touch on Dos and Don'ts later, but go forth and experiment. Especially in the beginning, nothing teaches us as quickly and thoroughly (and inexpensively) as trying something ourselves.

Choose a scene. Record it in a *sotto-voce* near-monotone. Record it again as if you're performing for *The Muppets* (Kermit's panic against Ms. Piggy's utter disdain). Next do it with all the self-seriousness of *The Avengers*. Somewhere in that middle ground, you'll start to discover how you want to sound.

Again:

Be willing to sound stupid!

It's awesome!

Record Your Voice

I hear your very first reaction: "I hate my recorded voice."

I have a very simple response to that: "Get over it!"

Seriously.

Most microphones are highly accurate devices. This has been true since the early 1900s. The sound of your voice as captured and reproduced on all but the cheapest devices is very close to how you sound.

More accurately, it's how you sound *to everyone other than yourself.*

There *is* a reason that you hate the sound of your

voice. Over 50% of your own voice is transmitted directly to your inner ear by vibrations traveling up your jawbone. Without that portion of direct transmission, your voice will sound just enough like you to feel terribly wrong!

I repeat: Get over it.

Yes, there are a few, rare, grating or piercing voices. Most of these can be fixed with vocal training or speech therapy. But unless people wince every time you open your mouth, that probably isn't you.

Two examples.

The first swears that no one would want to hear her voice reading her books. She has a lovely and expressive soft Texas accent and she writes romances set in, wait for it, Texas. I've been nudging her for three years to try doing her own audio—consider this another nudge.

The other is a nonfiction author who says, "I have a *nothing* New York voice." And while she's right in a way—her voice has none of the drama of the previous example—she is a passionate and popular public speaker on the topics about which she writes and consults.

I couldn't *imagine* a better narrator for either of their works.

Your voice *sounds* fine 99.999% of the time. It's the presentation that you need to work on.

3

Character Voices

Three Essential Rules

THIS SEEMS like a good place to start.

Rule #1: Keep your tone pleasant.

I don't mean that it has to be sweetness and light, but it has to be nice to listen to—for a long period of time (the length of a multi-hour audiobook).

The Wicked Witch of the West may have successfully scared the daylights out of little kids (and grown ones) ever since *The Wizard of Oz* premiered seventy years ago. "I'll get you, my pretty, and your little dog too." (Followed by mad cackling.) However, an entire audiobook in which the villain speaks in mad cackle…probably not so much.

Beginning male narrators often make this mistake when attempting to voice women. They go high, squeaky, nasal, and all sorts of other things that (a) women aren't, and (b) are irritating to listen to. Female narrators have a similar issue when trying to do a low, gravelly-voiced male. This will more typically end up overly breathy, and silly rather than irritating, but it still isn't a pleasant listen.

. . .

Rule #2: Under- rather than over-dramatize.

This is easy to prove to yourself. Take a few of those scenes that I suggested you record earlier (you did that, right?).

Listen to the blandly monotone one. It's listenable. It may not inspire (and yes, we *know* you hate your voice, get over it), but neither does it push you away.

Now listen to the wildly over-dramatic one. Do you lose the thread of the story (your own story!) because you were too wrapped up in the ridiculous Kermit-like drama? Could you listen to that for hours without heaving your player against the wall?

Yes, the middle balance is best, but overly dramatic is the worse choice, so this is a place to err on the side of caution.

Rule #3: KISS.

"Keep it simple, stupid." There's a reason that this has been the guiding principle of so many successful corporations. Especially in your first audiobooks, just like in your early writing, keeping it simpler is far more effective.

There are advanced writing techniques that I'm only now starting to get a grasp on after twenty-five years and sixty novels of writing fiction. After narrating thirty titles, I find this to be just as true of creating audiobooks. I've identified three general levels of narration skills below.

Level 1: Basics

This level of skill may seem over-simplified, but it isn't.

This is just the most basic technique that you need to get into your narrator's toolkit before you advance any further.

- Female character = highest voice (without going false)
- Female narrator = high voice
- Male narrator = low voice
- Male character = lowest voice (without going silly)

I started even simpler as a beginning narrator, with just three voices, making the male and female narrator the same "narrator" voice. I now use the variations as an additional cue to the listener as to whose point of view they're in.

The "narrator" voice is where the nonfiction writer always speaks.

In either case, fiction or nonfiction, I strongly recommend making the narrator's voice your natural speaking voice. First, it will sound like you. Second, it provides the least strain on your voice. Third, when you "fall out of voice" because you're tired or working on other aspects of narrating your book, you'll land naturally in your speaking voice, which is already the right voice.

All of your voices should fall within your natural vocal range. Practice can extend this range, but going false or squeaky, unless of course it's called for by the character, should be avoided.

Accents

This book does not address accents.

Partly because this isn't a class on accents.

There are numerous online resources for studying that.

Partly because, like the dramatic-ness aspect I mentioned above, getting it wrong is far more off-putting than not doing it at all.

And finally, because I suck at them. If you are a person who is good with accents, great, go for it. (I'm working with someone who wants to record her own books because there is a very, very specific regional accent that she feels is essential to the character, but no one who didn't grow up there would get it right.) Me? I'd never get it right.

Thankfully, the solution can be quite straightforward—it's probably already there in your book.

"Howdy," Captain Roberts moseyed up slower than his deep Texas drawl. "I'm lookin' for Stan but you, ma'am, are far too fine to be him."

The cue to his accent is right there on the written and narrated page, even if you don't end up giving the dialog itself much of a voice, we know he's proudly Texan.

Level Two: Written Attributes

The next level of skill for distinguishing a character's unique voice is less about voice and more about three other key techniques:

- Word choice
- Pacing
- Dynamics

The beauty of this set of tools is that you've already done all of the work on this while writing your manuscript. The challenge here is to bring what you put on the written page to life in the "spoken page."

Word choice is very straightforward. You created an erudite character who expresses itself with a certain degree of sophistication or a casual guy who just lays it out the way he sees it (and all the other variations). The word choice is already there.

But, if you're a truly organic writer, you may not be consciously aware of these choices.

Don't worry; you've already captured them in your writing.

Think instead of the way you've always felt this character spoke and let that take precedence.

Pacing is only a little more advanced. Did you ever tag a character as quick-witted or lugubrious or hesitant? These are your cues for how fast they speak and think (when they're the point-of-view narrator).

I created a character named Chelsea who speaks in long whirlwinds of dialogue that no one can interrupt. So, I read her fast and breathlessly. Another who is Rock of Gibraltar calm—his narrated voice is slow and thoughtful. Another, with a wry sense of humor always lurking beneath the surface, typically expresses himself with teasing rhetorical questions and a lighter tone than his military command voice.

You imagined all of your characters and how they spoke on the written page. Now is the time to risk sounding a little stupid in the privacy of your recording booth to discover how they speak. I'll try out character voices when I'm alone in the car, just to see how I can make them sound the same way they do in my head.

I labeled the last bullet point "dynamics" for a reason.

Are they loud-spoken or soft-spoken? But also, are they dynamically emotional and all over the map? Chelsea actually has a very narrow emotional spectrum—she's inimitably cheerful and can *always* find the bright side. Another character, suffering from PTSD, is likely to lapse from her calm, steady persona into tirades at a moment's notice, and finally collapse exhausted once she's been talked down and feels calmer.

Again, this is all information that is on the written page. Unflappable, highly educated, proud of his Okie roots, just a little naive so they always sound a bit surprised, etc.

Level Three: Advanced Voice Skills

This is where the fun is because the possibilities never end. I will offer a few pointers on where to start, but a true student of the audiobook will never be bored.

Let's start with the Basics list above, of a high female voice to a low male voice.

Pitch

Once you've determined the general range of your voice, you need to start working on maintaining a consistent pitch. If you have a story of three women, start working on consistently voicing them in high, middle, and low (for a woman) pitch.

Dialog is particularly good for practicing this. By working on conversation among the three women (or men), you are able to start separating their voices. When you can consistently do this, start to accelerate the conversation. Whether excited, angry, or some other emotion, try working on rapid-fire response times and getting the voices shifting properly between each other.

This is something that becomes easy with practice. Professional narrators—inherently less familiar with a work than the author—will often go through and highlight the different voices in different colors: yellow high, orange middle, and pale green low, or some other aid to tell them when to change to which voice.

I find that, with a little practice or one quick read-through to remind myself of a scene, that I can read accurately without such markings.

Accent

If you can perform accents, this is the time that comes to the fore as a good way to separate voices. When I do this with the few accents I have control of, it's a challenge to switch between them. A conversation between a German, a Texan, and a Jewish guy from Brooklyn will definitely keep even the most seasoned narrator on their toes.

To make this easier, I try to throw a little mental switch from one voice to the next and I often trigger this physically. For the German, I stand up straighter. For the Texan, I'll hook a thumb in a pocket of my pants, and for the Brooklyn Jew I'll slouch a little and wave a hand about while I'm narrating. If it's fast conversation, I may be standing up straight with one thumb hooked in a pocket and the other hand free to wave about, and then I shift my mental focus from one trigger to the next as I shift from one voice to the next.

Experiment! Find what works for you.

Chest to Head Voice

Go into your recording booth (which we'll talk about soon) or your car or wherever, and say the letter A in a sustained aaaaaaaaaa (not "ah"). Start as low as you can. Feel it in your chest or the base of your throat.

Now shift its tone slowly as you continue to make the A sound—a sliding tone that goes from low to middle and finally to a high note. You can think about singing it on a sliding scale if that helps. We're not after vocal perfection on the operatic stage here, so just give it a try.

As the tone shifts, notice where you feel it: chest, base of throat, back of throat, back of tongue, and then it may seem to climb forward along the roof of your mouth or even feel as if it's shifting up into your head.

Try this with other vowels just to get the feel for it.

Then try it with speech: start out talking like a grumpy Navy SEAL and end up sounding like a pixie.

The trick to using this tool is to then understand that a middle tone may feel like it's in the back of your throat—and perhaps that becomes your narrator. Pushing up to feeling as if it's at the base of your tongue may be your "high" female voice.

This is just another tool to help learn control of a character's particular voice and hopefully make it easier to reproduce time after time.

Breathiness

Try this. Say a simple phrase aloud, perhaps "Hello there." Now say it again but move your jaw much more or much less as you do so. This simple trick can change how breathy a voice sounds and shift its sound significantly.

Try Anything

By experimenting, you'll rapidly learn what affects your voice and what may or may not be useful. Speak with your shoulders back or hunched forward. Tip your head back or tip your chin down.

Here's another one. What if someone always speaks a little too softly or a little too loudly? You could, of course, do just that. But as you'll see when we get to discussing a few tips on best use of a microphone, you want to record everything as near the same volume as possible.

So, what do you do?

Speak softly but shift just a little closer to the microphone. It will record your voice more loudly because you're closer, but your voice will change just because you're speaking more softly, and the microphone will capture that. Pull back and speak more loudly—the microphone will pick up less of the stronger voice and balance it out. But again, it will capture the change in your voice.

Maybe now you can start to see why I said, *Be willing to sound stupid* earlier. I've thought about "silly" rather than stupid, but I want a more extreme reaction, especially when you're experimenting.

Do things that you *know* won't work...and maybe they will.

Study Narrators

Now is the time to return to listening to various audiobook narrators again. Start making notes about how the narrator handled every single one of the techniques above and more that I haven't listed here.

Why do this? Because the more you train yourself to hear, the more you can create and reproduce (or choose not to). Also, just like writing, various skills will become integrated into your subconscious as a narrator. Do you still think about what to include in dialog versus narration? For the most part, that's a beginning skill that you integrate automatically into your writing, except when you're trying to achieve something in particular.

Here's a partial checklist of things to study and learn from other narrators, storytellers, and actors.

- Pitch – both the primary pitch and degree of variation.
- Drama – how dramatic is one character versus another and how does the narrator handle this?
- Drama II – How much of an emotion (fear, excitement, passion) is shown by sounding that way (afraid, joyous, amorous) or is less better than more, offering cues but not drastically shifting the voice?
- Accent.
- Chest-to-head voice.
- Breathiness.
- How did their voice shift between male and female? Between dialog and narrative?
- How did the narrator handle a comma versus a period versus a paragraph break? Those three have successively longer silences.
- Are there parenthetical asides? How did the narrator shift their tone and pacing for that? (Try to mimic them, then try changing it up a couple of different ways. The real answer? Do an aside just as you would if you were making one while telling a story to a friend.)
- What else did they do to distinguish characters?
- To create tension?

In nonfiction, ask many of these same questions, except there is only one "character."

- How did the narrator vary their tone and pacing to keep your interest?
- Are examples or explanations voiced differently than the primary text?
- How did they vary the pacing to keep your attention? Especially pay attention to introduction and summary paragraphs.
- How did they handle charts, diagrams, and photographs? To narrate these, I'll often write a supplementary paragraph and insert it into the narration. Without the visual element available, I consider why I included that particular graphic or image and will narrate the key elements of that. "Imagine" is a very useful word in this case, even as simple as "Imagine a pie. Forty percent of that would be consumed by…" Or is the information sufficiently explained in the text that you may simply skip the graphic entirely.

Memoir is a specialized case of nonfiction. Extra care must be taken to keep the story engaging. Why? Because it is your own story. Probably built from tales you've often told to others over the years. Focus particularly on how the narrator varies the energy of the presentation: upbeat, thoughtful, cautionary, amused, etc.

Your Voice

Now, having pushed you to study as much as possible, STOP!

Seriously.

Whenever you listen to an audiobook in the future (or a play or a good presenter), you'll hear so much more than you did before.

Now it's time to start finding your *own* voice.

In writing, the one thing you can't hear at all is your own writing voice. And, for the most part, that's what makes a reader into a fan. Someone falls in love with *your* writing voice. (There's a strong argument against excessive editing of your manuscript: it is dangerously easy to edit your voice out of the book because *you* can't hear it. There are people who can do this type of editing without killing their voice, and I'm in awe of them. I always approach my second and third drafts with great caution and a little trepidation.)

Your narrator voice has a similar concern, it needs to match your writing voice—more specifically, *your* voice. That voice that only you of all people can't hear.

How do you find your voice if you can't hear it?

First, once you've trained your narrating skills, you need to *stop* studying other voices. You want to learn technique, but you don't want to become a mimic. Yes, you'll continue to learn new things as you listen to new narrators, storytellers, and actors, but it's time to stop studying for now.

Second, practice. Narrating your own work will naturally lead you toward your own voice.

Trust the process.

Get to work.

4

The Recording Space

THERE ARE certain preconceptions about recording spaces. (I'm not calling it a booth to try and help break those.) How many videos / movies have we seen of recording artists with the headphones, fancy microphone, backup band, and clear glass to a console that is a dial manufacturer's wet dream?

If you're producing the next hit album, sure, go for it.

Otherwise, let's get real. You need a microphone and enough room to fit you in front of it. My most expensive booth cost me sixty-five dollars. My current one cost me under ten (if I'd bought everything new, which I didn't).

The Two Purposes

A recording space serves two purposes:

1. Keep the outside world's sounds outside.
2. Provide an acoustically "dead" space for recording.

The first purpose is obvious and that's what the rest of this chapter will be about.

But let's take a moment to properly understand the second purpose.

Dead Space (also called "Room Liveliness")

Step outside or into a truly big room.

Clap your hands once. Or snap your fingers.

It sounds like you just clapped your hands (or snapped your fingers). Nothing much going on.

Now go into your bathroom or any other small room and try to do it with the same force.

Suddenly there's a great deal going on. Not only does it seem louder; it seems brighter and snappier.

What's happening is that when you clapped your hands outside, all you heard was the little bit of sound that was aimed at you. In all other directions, the sound just spilled away out into the world for others to enjoy.

Your bathroom (filled with flat surfaces like walls, tiles, and shower-stall glass) reflected much of the rest of that sound back to you. It bounces it around, especially the higher pitched (brighter) tones. That room is said to be very lively or reactive to sound.

This sucks for audio recording.

In fact, about the best studio space available is the great outdoors—except it's never quiet. Traffic, ocean surf, airplanes, birds, wind… It's a major battle for movie makers who actually solve this by re-recording most voices as lip syncs in carefully isolated studios. (On major movies, there always seems to be one or two actors who suck at lip sync, so they are very carefully recorded during initial filming. I was talking to a friend who saw some actual shooting footage for an early Star Wars movie. All the voices were muffled or unclear—except Carrie Fisher's. Hers was always perfect because she couldn't lip sync well.)

So, one of the major tasks of a recording space, after we've blocked out the outside world, is to not end up in too lively a room. Thankfully, this is very easy to achieve.

Assessing a Space

You need to locate an area that is at least 3' x 4' (you can go smaller, but it typically isn't much fun). You don't actually need more space, though there are a few reasons to go a little bigger if you can. Mostly to avoid claustrophobia and to get better air circulation. But it won't significantly affect the sound.

The space should be as isolated as possible from outside noises. If you live in the country or one of our other low-population areas, this is less difficult. The more urban your environment, the greater the challenges.

If you live on an isolated piece of property, a guest bedroom can be easily converted or even a corner of the living room. I have a friend who double-insulated the front six feet of his trailer home. He can even record in campgrounds, as long as no one is running a generator too close by.

In noisier environments, interior rooms are the best bet. Master closets, bathrooms, and basements all can serve well. Go stand in one, close the door, and listen.

- Is there a nearby road from which passing trucks cause deep-note vibrations? If you live alone or have a tolerant spouse, perhaps you can record at night when the road goes quiet. (Let me just say that nearby construction sucks and I can seriously empathize with your pain.)

- Are the noises soft enough that they won't be an issue? We'll get to this.
- What about other noises? Do you have kids? Can they play at the far side of the house or can you record while they're at day care? Teenagers who you can buy headphones for?
- Or maybe there's another space that solves some issues, but not others. Perhaps recording in the basement after everyone goes to bed so that the floor isn't creaking into the microphone every time someone moves.

I'm going to review five possible booths below (three of which were mine) to help you solve this for yourself.

Space #1 - The Master Closet

I've seen an identical setup in a front hall coat closet, but I had the luxury of a 6' x 8' master closet.

A clothes closet of any type has the advantage of already being filled with piles of soft, sound-absorbing fabrics that both insulate unwanted sounds from the outside world and dampen the brightness of the live recording.

We'll talk about equipment in the next chapter but suffice it to say that I use a foldable music stand set flat to hold up my computer and a boom microphone stand—and not much else.

I piled up our extra blankets and sweaters on the shelf around the room. Then I took an old blanket and tacked it across the inside of the closet door to dampen the reflections off that surface. I could have gone all out and tacked a flannel sheet across the ceiling to block that surface, but it was really overkill, so I didn't bother.

Space #2 - The Coat Rack

For six months I rented an apartment that had no room I could convert. The half bathroom was literally too small. Even sitting on the toilet, my knees were practically touching the door. The master bath was tiled floor, walls, and ceiling, there would be no tacking up blankets without a masonry drill.

The main bedroom was relatively well isolated from road noise, but it was a very bright-sounding room with lots of angles that would be difficult to muffle.

So, I bought one of those two-rod rolling coat racks ($50) and a piano stool ($15). With my piano stool at one end of the coat rack, my music stand / table at the other, and my mic boom sticking in from outside, I had a very cozy recording space.

To deaden it, I draped blankets and quilts over the coat rods and ended up with a fine (if a little hot and stuffy) recording space. Every time I had to pause a recording, I'd flap one of the openings to let in some fresh air.

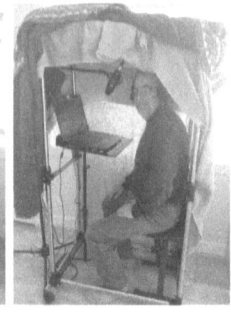

Space #3 - The Bathroom

My third and current booth is set up in a small, upstairs bathroom that's at the very center of the house, isolating it well from outside noises. The space between the shower stall and the door is just three by four feet.

With the insertion of a couple of small screw hooks into wall studs (creating holes little bigger than a picture hook), and the judicious use of the shower head and a towel hook, I hung a clothesline at six and a half feet high. I tied it so that it follows the outline of the small space.

Using clothespins and two blankets, I can convert it from a bathroom to a recording space in about five minutes. I also flop a piece of cloth over the top so that I'm completely inside a cloth box as I stand on the bathroom rug.

This is actually my favorite recording booth to date.

The acoustics are excellent.

Only two sounds easily penetrate the booth: a motorcycle passing on the road outside, and the central air heater / AC. I've learned to record on weekday mornings when there are very few motorcycles passing. And on the particularly cold or hot days, I crank the temperature a couple of degrees in the right direction, then switch it off for a while.

And whenever I'm taking a break (such as finishing a chapter and setting up the next one), I just flick on the bathroom fan and it sucks in a whole room of fresh air in moments.

Space #4 - The Bedroom

A bedroom can actually be a very good recording space acoustically if you live in a quiet area.

Use a cloth hanging above the head of your bed. Close the curtains. Perhaps drape a sheet (flannel works even better) over any big pictures or even the dresser. Throw a bunch of extra pillows all higgledy-piggledy onto the bed.

Stand at the foot of your bed facing the head of your bed.

Clap your hands.

The result is a surprisingly *unlively* space.

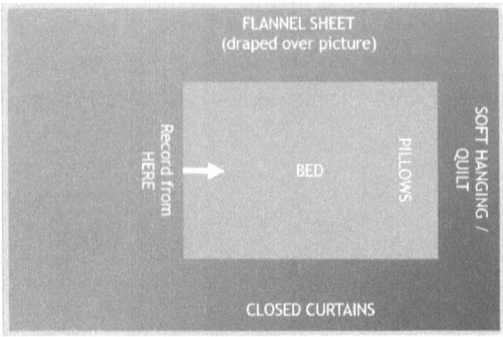

Space #5 - The Studio

There are numerous plans available online for this to fit every need, from prefabricated kits (of varying usefulness) to full-on, build-your-own plans. Just search on "Home recording booth."

I helped a friend research and build one of these. His challenge was that his business office and planned recording space was close by a highway. Not an interstate, but a major truck route that runs along the Oregon Coast. At the crest of a hill, the trucks were always laboring hard and the motorcycles that cruise this lovely highway only exacerbated the issue.

We tried various tricks to isolate a back room, but it just wasn't working. So, we built a 6' x 6' booth in there. It was a room within a room. Staggered wall studs, so that sound wasn't conducted through the walls. Packed insulation in the walls and ceiling. He, by plan, built the ceiling strongly enough to store an entire layer of filled book boxes on top —an absolute sound barrier.

The inside was completely lined with acoustical or "egg" foam. A desk was installed (with a piece of thick felt spread over it), and he was up and running. The booth needs to be retrofitted with a sound-insulating, silent fan system for sessions longer than half an hour—he built it so tightly that no fresh air could slip in. Otherwise, it's an amazing booth.

Space #6 - The Rental Booth

There are rental studios in many, many towns. Search on "Recording Studio Rental."

You can rent studio space in a pre-built studio booth often in the range of $20/hour. Some even have the equipment, though I would tend to use my own simply for consistency's sake.

Recording Spaces Sound Different

Every recording space will have its own sound. One will absorb more of the high tones. Another may emphasize lower tones.

We'll talk more about this in a later chapter on Engineering, but for now, understand that each recording space will require different engineering settings. Different equipment (the next chapter) will also have different sounds, though thankfully recording equipment is relatively space-independent.

For these reasons, if at all possible, use the same equipment in the same space for the entire duration of an audiobook narration to achieve the most consistent sound throughout the recording.

I have used seven different booths over the last eight years (sometimes doing just a single project for a friend) and I'm always surprised at how different they are acoustically.

Recording Sessions

I am not some marathon, professional narrator. Both I and my voice get tired after about two hours. Knowing this, I pre-plan for two-hour sessions.

I try to record the entire audiobook during sessions on consecutive days because it's the best way to keep the characters' narrated voices clear in my head.

I also keep the sessions short because I'm a writer, and my priority is writing every day, not recording.

5

Equipment

THE NUMBER One question I get? *What microphone should I buy?*

It both is and isn't that simple.

There are actually three key pieces in this part of the acoustic chain: computer, software, and microphone. Thankfully they are all easy to explain.

Computer

Your computer has two requirements.

First, it must be capable of running modern audio software. Audio takes much more capability than word processing.

My 80,000-word book is:

- 380 K in Microsoft Word.
- 2–4 MB in e-book and PDF formats.
- 750 MB in finished MP3 audio files ready for distribution.

- Worse, it's 6 GB in its raw, recorded WAV formatted files.
- And I maintain four different copies of those WAV files totaling almost 25 GB for the complete audio book.

Your computer must have the horsepower to process these giant files.

The good news is that audio isn't video or games. Any full computer under five years old with 4–8 MB of memory is probably up to the task. If you have a Chromebook or some other computer designed to run primarily online, sorry, you'll need an upgrade.

Second, your computer must be dead quiet in two ways: fan and keyboard.

Most laptops (and iMacs) meet the fan requirement.

If you have a desktop computer, the fan will be too loud but there is a simple solution. Purchase extender cables for your monitor, keyboard, and mouse and place the desktop outside the studio space, slipping the cables in under the door.

The biggest problem is typically the keyboard. Again, the solution is easy as so many devices are now touch-enabled (both laptops and tablets).

Because my laptop's keyboard is silent, I'm able to run both the recording software and my manuscript side by side on a single screen. Many professional readers will use the keyboard and monitor to control the recording software but have their manuscript on a tablet. I know of one studio that simply issues an iPad to every narrator it hires. This allows completely silent progress from one page to the next as they record.

Software (DAW - Digital Audio Workstation)

In Chapter 1 we discussed the option of recording and engineering your audiobook or just doing the recording, then contracting out the engineering.

If you are doing both, there is little choice in today's market—use Adobe Audition.

It's not that there aren't other choices, some even significantly more powerful, but for the task of recording and engineering an audiobook, there is simply no better tool available today. The combination of highly flexible tools, the ease of automating repetitive tasks, and reasonable price is untouched. (I tested over twenty DAWs before settling on Audition. Then I began talking to professional audiobook studios about my process and every single one agrees that for an audiobook, currently there is nothing better. There are more expensive DAWs, but for even the most complex audiobooks, they aren't needed. Audiobooks are very simple acoustically.)

Multiple-voice Narration

If you want to have multiple narrators (male and female roles or full cast), you will want a multiple-microphone setup. These are readily available, simply more expensive as you add more microphones.

In your recording software, you will want to record each voice on a separate track (Audition calls this Multitrack). It allows the recording of all of the microphones to merge into the same file with the same timing but allows each track to be adjusted separately.

This will vastly simplify the process of balancing

stronger and weaker voices and engineering each to its best quality. They can be recorded together or separately, but you'll want them all together in the same Multitrack file.

Currently, Adobe Audition is only available as part of a monthly subscription. If you're already using Adobe InDesign, Photoshop, or Acrobat, the chances are it's already included in your subscription. If you aren't subscribing to Adobe, it's worth it. The rental is also month-to-month, so if you aren't working on audio that month, you can switch it off.

Everything in the engineering chapter of this book will assume that you are using Adobe Audition, though the concepts can be transferred to any other equally capable platform.

That last phrase is key: *equally capable platform.*

There are a number of less expensive and even free audio processing tools. These tools will have a very high time cost, some requiring hours to achieve what Audition can do in seconds. Others store and process files in such a fashion that prior work may not be recoverable if an error occurs. (Which is another reason to save every version, but you can still lose hours of engineering if you aren't careful.)

Recording Only

If you are only doing the recording and are outsourcing the engineering, you may consider using a free or inexpensive tool for the recording itself. Even recording several books, then pay for a month of Audition to process them all at once.

There are a number of possible pitfalls here. For example, if you have to re-record a section, you'll have to go back to your original software to get a consistent result.

However, free is a very attractive word. At present, I would look at GarageBand for the Mac or Audacity for Windows.

Again, engineer on any cheap or free platform at your own risk.

The Microphone

At last, huh?

There are two primary types of microphones that we care about in the home audio environment (there are dozens of types and hundreds or even thousands of models of microphones). For us, it boils down to USB digital versus powered cardioid microphones. (A headset mike is not a good solution. Audiobook quality isn't like dictation quality.)

USB DIGITAL

The USB digital *seems* like an obvious choice. Plug a USB cable into your microphone, plug the other end into your computer, open your software, and go.

If only it were so simple.

There are many fine USB digital microphones—and if you notice carefully, most of them are labeled "Excellent for podcasting." We're back to that earlier quality question. For a podcast, a microphone needs to capture the voice well and clearly, and nothing else really matters.

In audio there's a concept called "signal-to-noise ratio."

What it means is: how much louder is the signal you want to capture than the inherent hiss, amplifier gain, and other noises that occur in the process of capturing those sound waves and making them digital. As long as a podcast is well above the noise floor, you're in good shape.

But remember our friend with the $400 headphones? She can hear that irritating noise floor easily. She may not care while listening to a podcast, but she probably will on an audiobook. Knowing this, audiobook distributors like ACX, Author's Republic, Findaway Voices, and others set much more stringent signal-to-noise requirements for audiobooks than would ever be necessary for a podcast.

USB Direct microphones are capable of achieving this, usually. Sometimes…maybe. I ultimately ended up giving mine away.

Powered Cardioid Microphone

Because these aren't relying on very low-power electronics, these microphones don't need to be run near their limits to achieve desired signal levels. Their signal-to-noise ratios are excellent even at moderate volumes. This technology (called phantom power) has been around for exactly a hundred years as of 2019 and is still the standard in studios, on stage, and in the very best microphones in the world.

Simple tip when shopping: the powered microphone's cable has a big round plug on either end with three prongs in it. Never a flat USB cable. Also, the amplifier must have "USB output." That's so that you can plug it into your computer.

Choosing a Microphone

So, how to choose among the hundreds of powered cardioid microphones that are available becomes the next challenge. Oddly enough, quality plays in our favor this time.

Yes, you can spend $10,000 or more on a Neumann microphone that will dazzle in what it can capture. I recently spoke to a friend who was doing a major anniversary recording for Seattle Opera. Neumann was so interested in how their microphones would perform in such an environment that they sent a pair (stereo) of specially hand-tuned microphones to Seattle for him to use. Of course, at over $20,000 apiece, they didn't ship them—they flew them up with the technician who would be the only one actually allowed to touch them. The result was indeed incredible.

However, we aren't capturing a stageful of world-class singers, a seventy-piece orchestra, and the acoustics of one of the newest and finest opera houses in America.

We're recording a single voice narrating a book.

Almost any good quality voice microphone will perform the task.

At this writing, I like the Focusrite Scarlett 2i2 Studio. For under $250, I get a good, voice-friendly microphone, the powered amplifier, decent headphones, and both of the necessary cables. Done!

Want to research other options? The phrase to search on is "voice-over microphone," not "podcasting microphone."

ACCESSORIES

The shock mount ($15–$20).

This is an essential accessory. Many microphones ship with only a standard clip or screw-on mount. A shock mount suspends the microphone within the mount with what are essentially rubber bands. This drastically cuts the noises that can be transmitted directly into the microphone by such things as bumps against the microphone stand, or even the low rumble of a passing truck being transmitted up through the flooring. Caution: the shock mount size must match the microphone shaft size, be careful if ordering separately (44 mm and 54 mm are two common standards).

Pop filter ($10–$20).

This is the other very popular accessory.

Here's why you need one.

Hold your palm up within a couple inches of your face: palm facing you, fingertips at eye level, and your wrist in front of your chin.

Say, "Pop!" Note the blast of air that splashed against your palm.

Say, "Foof!" Note the air that runs along your wrist.

If either of those hit the microphone, it will sound as if you thumped your microphone with a hard finger flick. Very uncomfortable to listen to and very hard to fix in post-recording.

A pop filter is a fine mesh screen designed to stop the blast of air but not hamper the sound passing through the screen from reaching your microphone.

Here's why you *don't* need one.

One day, after I'd hit my pop filter for about the tenth time in my tiny recording space, I wondered how I could get rid of it. Then I remembered a photo of an old live radio show. A group of performers—I think it was The Weavers with Pete Seeger—gathered around a microphone dangling from above, hung at the height of their foreheads.

Most good voice-over microphones are called cardioid or hyper-cardioid, meaning that they pick up best from one side (typically marked with a circle, a heart, or the manufacturer's logo). So, I wanted that aimed directly at my mouth, but out of the way of my p's and f's.

It took a little fooling around, but I raised the boom and placed the microphone upside down, so that the mount is highest and very close to my forehead (less than an inch when recording). I angle the microphone itself down and away from me so that the center of the front is aimed at my mouth from just inches beyond my nose. I place it right at the upper edge of my sightline to my computer screen.

Suddenly all of my "pops" and "foofs" passed below the microphone rather than impacting its very sensitive diaphragm. It actually placed the pickup element closer to my mouth than when it was behind the pop filter. It is not a typical setup, but I don't miss the awkward pop filter and I've been very happy with the results.

Setting Up Your Microphone

The sound of your voice travels into the microphone, which turns it into an electronic analog signal (don't worry about the meaning of analog—if you care, it means varying voltage rather than the 1s and 0s of digital). The amplifier turns the analog signal into a digital one and then sends it to your computer over the USB.

However, before the signal can reach the audio software, it's going to run into the computer's operating system first. The first time you plug it in, your computer will take a minute or so to set it up.

So far, all good.

There's one little crucial control, the operating system's volume control.

In Windows, right-click on the small speaker icon in

the System Tray (lower right corner). The top option will be "Open Volume Mixer." (If it's an old enough version to say "Recording," you want that option.) When you select that, you'll see the name of your microphone, amplifier, or its manufacturer.

Now comes the fun part. You want to adjust the volume of that up or down until, speaking in a normal, narration voice, the software (which we'll talk about in detail below) records your voice strongly. That lies in the -3 to -18 dB range and which Audition is kind enough to mark in yellow. We want to avoid sending it too much into the red or losing it into the lower parts of the green.

The "Weird Little Echo" Tip

If you hear an echo of yourself over your headphones as you're trying to record (one that is just completely and maddeningly delayed from your actual narration), hopefully this tip or some variation of it will solve your problem. (I record on Windows, so I can't speak to whether this is an issue on the Mac or how to fix it, but I suspect the solution is similar.)

What's happening is that you're listening to both the microphone amplifier and the delayed monitor feedback from the headphone amplifier.

Reopen the Volume Mixer control by right-clicking on the small speaker icon at the lower right of your screen.

The name of your amplifier probably appears twice. Click Mute on the right-hand one. That should solve the echo.

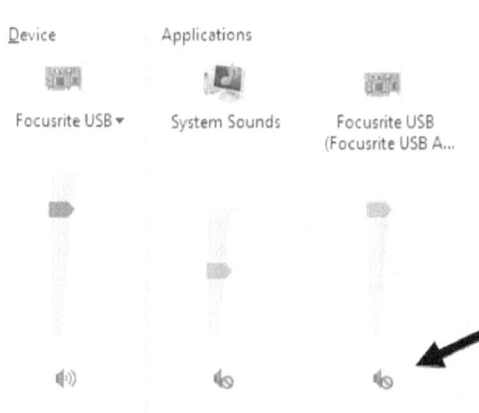

Three Simple Microphone Techniques

These are three simple techniques that will vastly improve the quality and enjoyability of your recording.

DISTANCE VS. VOLUME

Watch a professional singer and how they use a microphone. In fact, if you're a fan of *The Voice*, watch the blind auditions. Knowing this simple trick, you can immediately see the professionals who are most likely to be chosen.

The moment they punch out a big note, they pull the microphone away. Yet it still sounds amazing.

What's going on here?

They know that they have such big voices that they can easily overwhelm the microphone and the electronics with raw voice power. So, to get that big note, they back away. (There's a little more than this going on having to do with limiters and clipping, but I only mention that to satisfy the true audio geeks.)

Translating this technique into the audiobook booth, how do you have a character shout in surprise or warning, and make it sound authentic? You don't try to shout softly. Instead, you back away. If I want to make a really "big" sound, I'll even turn my face away from the microphone toward one of the blankets that make up my recording space's walls.

This allows me to project the volume in a way that will reshape the voice into a shout but end up with the same amount of signal when it reaches the recording software.

The same is true of a whisper.

I'll whisper softly, with all the breathiness that entails, but I'll move very close to the microphone. Again, I'll end up with a strong signal and good clarity. But it will sound like I'm whispering.

Sounding Far Away

This is actually a variation on the same theme. Speak normally and move away. It doesn't take much. Six inches or a foot is plenty for most effects.

In order to sound very close, a slightly different technique is required. I move in toward the microphone but turn my face slightly aside. Why? Those dreaded p's and f's. I want them off to the side of the microphone.

Record With Headphones

Microphones, even narrowly focused hyper-cardioid ones, pick up everything. And I mean *everything!* Tongue clicks, air bubbles popping in your throat, when you swallow excess saliva (back away from the microphone or tap pause to do this), keyboard clicks, my wife downstairs putting a dish in the sink, everything.

Thankfully, the softer the noise, the easier it is to fix. The latter ones are wiped out by the settings in the engineering chapter, the first couple—along with passing motorcycles—not so much.

Some of these louder sounds, especially the sharp clicks and pops, are relatively easy to fix in the engineering process, which we'll discuss when we get there. But what about the metallic bump when you accidentally knocked your hand against the music stand?

By recording with headphones, you'll hear what the microphone hears. If it's enough to draw your attention, you probably need to stop, back up, and re-record that section. It will save you a lot of heartache later.

6

A Recording Session

The Voice Bible

WE ALL KNOW what a story bible is: a way for tracking all of the character and factual details about your story. Because accidentally demoting a soldier's rank from the prior book when it's finally her turn to have a romance is really unkind. (Having done it, I know and…my fans picked it up and… sigh!)

So, you finally have determined what you want your characters' voices to sound like. But how do you keep track of them—from one recording session to the next, from one book to the next?

Create a Voice Bible.

Start recording, and briefly describe each character's voice in the correct tone and pace and whatever else you've worked out.

Sample Voice Bible

Henderson's Ranch #8, *Big Sky Dog Whisperer* (from low-to-high, from male-to-female)

"Stan is a big-chested SEAL with a deep voice. His sentences are short and he's very hard to upset. Mark is almost as deep-voiced as Stan but always has a small twist of humor unless he slips into ultra-serious command mode, then he's abrupt and sharply punctuated. Michael speaks softly. His voice would never stand out in a crowd. The male narrator falls about here. Patrick actually speaks higher than the male narrator. He's easy-going and casual, from Long Island with a bit of fake Texas. Ama is the matriarch and speaks as deep in the chest as Stan, but with no vibration, it's all on the breath. Eternally calm, she is the voice of wisdom. The female narrator is here. Jodi is just above the female narrator in pitch. Her tone is short, sharp, declarative sentences except when she's pissed, then her voice goes up in speed and takes on a slightly hysterical edge as she has PTSD. Emily is even-toned, with very little dynamic variation. Her head is back, and she speaks from the back of her throat with a little breathiness. Chelsea is up here, always fast, always cheerful, always stringing thoughts together faster than anyone can possibly follow them."

Before each recording session, the first thing I'll do is listen to that book's / series' Voice Bible recording to get all of the character voices back in my head. As a beginning narrator, I kept the Voice Bible open in the background so that I could jump over and brush up on the voice of someone about to enter the scene.

After thirty titles, I rarely need to relisten to a Voice Bible once I've built it the first time. Why? Because I've gotten better at making them sound the way they are in my writer's head.

Thinking While Recording

One of the most advanced techniques of recording an audiobook—and perhaps the most difficult step of the entire process—is thinking about a large number of things simultaneously while recording. Again, practice is key here.

Here's the terrifying (initially) list of what I now track while narrating. Did I keep track of all this in my first recordings? Not a chance. It's a learned skill that requires patience.

VOICING

- Proper characterization and pacing per the above discussions.
- Over-enunciation. Most of us are, by nature, lazy speakers. An audiobook is all about understanding the words, often in harsh listening environments such as cars or over headphones while exercising. Enunciate carefully without sounding pedantic.
- Correct pronunciation. That word that you always just type but never think about, look it up. (Ex: Do you say pro*noun*ciation or pro*nun*ciation? Second one is right.) Go listen to that French phrase or Scottish lord's name, that you tossed in so casually as a writer, *before* you record it.

Pronunciation Recording Tips:

Go through your manuscript beforehand. Look up each tricky pronunciation and write it phonetically next to the word in your reading manuscript.

I'll pause the recording right before a tricky phrase, go online and listen to it several times, then jump in and record it while the sounds, pacing, and syllable stresses are fresh in my memory.

For names, search online starting with: "How to say…" or "How to pronounce…" will find great collections of very short videos. Some of them are now computer-generated rather than human spoken. I try to double-check those against a human voice or dictionary when I hear them.

Recording

We'll talk about both of these shortly, but they need to be mentioned here as they are something to pay attention to as you're recording.

- Watch for bad spikes in volume. It's easier to fix them right away.
- Extraneous sounds. This is why you record wearing headphones.

Presentation

- Voice and energy levels. It is very easy to fall into rote reading of a manuscript. Your voice's volume goes down and the energy goes flat. It requires constant vigilance to keep your energy lively throughout the course of an audiobook. We'll get into some tips on doing this at the very end.
- Have fun! This is perhaps the key element of a successful audiobook narration. It's said that if you aren't having fun with your writing, your reader can "hear" it in your written words. If you aren't having fun narrating your audio, they can hear it far more easily in your voice. Audio narration must be enjoyable to listen to, and the best way to achieve that is to enjoy the process of recording and bringing your book to life in the spoken word.

Do I attempt to do all of this simultaneously? Absolutely not!

Instead I break it down into: what do I do continuously, and what do I just need to "check in on" as I go.

All the time

- Characterization and pacing.
- Pronunciation.
- Extraneous noises (these are easy because you'll hear them over your headphones).

Every minute or so

- Am I enunciating carefully?
- How's my energy/fun level?

Either as I go or at the end of each chapter

- A quick glance to find the bad peak sounds to fix.

Tip: Try to breathe quietly and often. Taking numerous smaller breaths will help you not run out of breath. And while your breathing will never be silent, if you can avoid loud gulps, it will save your engineer significant time.

The Recording Session

No dairy

Don't eat or drink any dairy for at least an hour prior to recording. It coats your throat and makes it harder to enunciate clearly. It also clings to surfaces inside your mouth and causes air bubbles (which pop and the microphone picks up really, really well).

Highly carbonated beverages will *feel* as if they scour your throat clean, but they also cause your muscles to tighten up.

The best thing to drink during a recording session? Highly diluted lemonade or water with lemon squeezed into it. This will do the best job of keeping your throat clear.

. . .

Warm up your voice

Just like warming up before a workout. Your voice will be, and more importantly sound, more agile and lively.

There are numerous exercises online for warming up your voice. Making high and low sounds, sliding pitch scales, humming strongly, singing scales, repeating complex phrases, and many more.

My favorite warmup? Reading aloud with my Voice Bible playing over the headphones. It plants the feeling of those characters back in my body as well as my voice.

Isolate

Get into a space of isolation—both mentally and physically. As mentioned above, there is a great deal to focus on while making a recording. You can't do this while thinking about anything else. Not picking up the kid, what's for dinner, or the next scene from that morning's writing session.

It is essential to set all other thoughts and concerns aside—they belong outside the recording booth, not in it.

Record

Recording is the easiest technical task of the entire audiobook process. Literally, just click record.

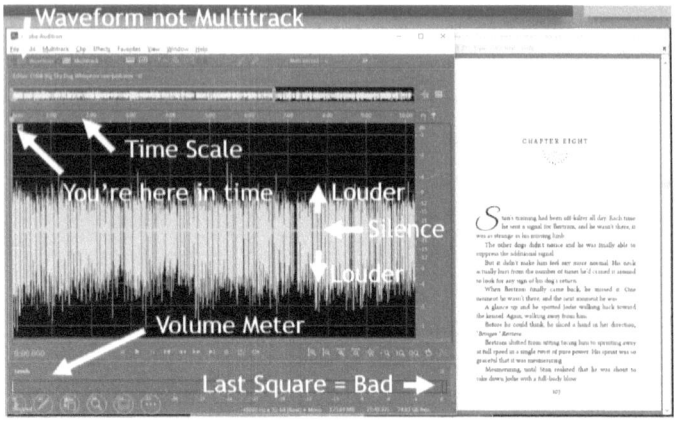

Understanding a DAW Screen

A Digital Audio Workstation (DAW = audio processing software) is unlike any other software. Time begins at zero at the left and moves to the right. There is a time scale to show this. A thin band, like a miniaturized version of the main screen, will show how much of the file you are viewing and make it easy to zoom in and out.

The central line is dead silence. Sound is a wave, and is literally represented that way, swinging above and below this central line. It isn't louder or softer if it is above or below the line, it is simply the shape of the sound. The *amount* (amplitude) that it is above or below this line represents its volume. If it passes up or down out of the box, passing the 0 dB mark (zero decibels, a measure of loudness), it's bad (called clipping) and will need re-recording.

I typically lay out the amplitude (volume) level meter across the bottom. Recording in the upper green and yellow is good. Recording in the red is time to be cautious. If you light up the last little square, it will stay lit until you click it to clear it. It means that you clipped badly and *must* re-record.

Errors While Recording

There are three ways to manage errors made while recording: Clap-it, Cut-in, or Punch-and-roll.

Clap-it

The idea here is that you never stop recording.

When you make an error (stumbling over a phrase, using the wrong voice, whatever), clap your hands close in front of the microphone. This will place a big, obvious spike on the recording for the engineer to find.

Continue narrating, starting from a sentence before your mistake.

Mess up again? Clap again.

Keep this up until you have a complete and clean recording, excepting the mistakes and their matching claps.

Now, during the engineering phase of the process, the engineer (potentially you) will see the big spike, know there's an error, and simply delete the bad version(s).

I do *not* recommend this method (left over from the days of rolling tape) for several reasons:

- Your "claps" will mask the occasional bad spike of clipping elsewhere in the file.
- It doesn't allow your voice to rest.
- You will be shifting the time cost to fix it down to the engineer and will delay them far longer than it would delay you to use either of the next two methods to fix it right away.

Personally, I know exactly where the error is in

the recording because I just made it; so, I fix it and move on.

Cut-in

This refers to halting the recording, backing up to just before the error (typically at the end of the preceding paragraph or sentence), then restart the recording and continuing where you cut in. When you're done, you will have a single, complete, clean recording.

Tip: While the recording is paused is an excellent moment to take a sip of water. Keeping your throat well hydrated is very important.

Punch-and-roll

This marvelous and advanced tool was only recently added to Adobe Audition and audio geeks everywhere are…geeking. (Audacity has it; and the last time I checked, GarageBand can be fooled into thinking it kind of does.)

Once you've backed up to the end of a clean section, you align the cursor just as you did for the Cut-in method. However, instead of simply starting the recording and guessing at how long to make the gap before the start of the next word, Punch-and-roll holds your hand.

It scrolls back and plays the last five seconds of your clean section, then, when the playback reaches where you placed your cursor, the software automatically switches over to record. You can easily hear the volume and pacing, then simply start narrating to record in just the right place. Wonderful!

Keyboard Shortcuts

There are a few Adobe Audition keyboard shortcuts that will make your life so much easier.

space = play / stop

shift + space = record

shift + alt + space = punch-and-roll record

cursor right and left = move in time (when recording is paused)

+ / - (plus / minus) = expand / contract zoom

What to Record

All audio needs to be separated into at least four files:

Front Matter

- Title (and subtitle)
- Series name and number (if a series)
- Written and narrated by (you)
- Foreword / dedication (if any)

Chapters

- As many of these as you have chapters. Though a short story may be tucked all into one file if it's under 18,000 words.
- Maximum of one chapter per file.
- If you are starting a new section or part, you

must read that aloud. The audio should match the book as much as possible.

Back Matter

- Title
- Series name and number (if a series)
- Written and narrated by
- Title and performance copyright (year)
- All rights reserved
- Marketing info. For example: "For more information about this and other titles, please visit www.mlbuchman.com, that's m-l-b-u-c-h-m-a-n dot com."
- "Thank you for listening."

Sample of Audiobook

- Maximum of 5 minutes long; best is 3–5 minutes.
- Typically, the opening of chapter one without any chapter number or title.
- Trim to a good cliffhanger point, as this will be all they can hear without buying the audiobook. Entice them in.
- You don't need to record this; you just snip it out of your chapter one recording and save it as "Sample."

A word on the marketing section: *Think like a listener.* When you've finished listening to an audiobook, do you keep listening? About the author, about the publisher, a list of other titles in the series, and…

I certainly don't.

However, if the listener can see that they're just thirty or so seconds from the end, maybe they'll let it play out. Or they're going through a tricky intersection in their car and can't jump to the next book right away.

Therefore, I made the decision to keep my marketing trimmed down to the phrases above. I don't even include an excerpt of the next title to hook them back in. Though I've considered it, I still like the lean and clean information above.

Always, always, always thank your listener. They gave you their money and their time. That's major.

Silence, Length, and Other Tech

There are a couple of silence requirements in a finished recording that are best prepared for by, you guessed it, recording some silence. Don't worry about exact timings while recording, but if you leave some silence in these places, it will make it very simple to edit their length during engineering.

To meet today's distributors' standards, silence is required as follows:

- 0.5–1.0 seconds prior to any audio in a file (I use 0.5).
- 2.5 seconds between chapter number / name and the start of text (good rule of thumb).
- 1.0–5.0 seconds at end of each audio file (3.5 seconds recommended, otherwise the text at the end of one chapter's file will breathlessly bump straight into the chapter number of the next).
- I also count to four slowly for scene breaks. I like the feel of four seconds for that break.

The only other significant rule is that no one file may be over 120 minutes (2 hours) long. That's about 18,000 words—a very long chapter.

If you research online, you'll find numerous requirements for noise floors, total RMS, and parameters. If you follow the steps in this book, they should all take care of themselves as part of the process with no extra effort by you.

Words Per Hour

An audiobook should be read at approximately 9,000 words per hour. Much slower will actually be irritating to the listener and much faster can decrease comprehension and enjoyment. Yes, there are the time-pressed among us who will listen to audio at a zoomed rate, but that needs to be the listener's choice.

So, how do you set that ideal narration pace? Imagine that you're telling a story, which conveniently you are, and want to keep your audience engaged. That's pretty much spot on.

For a more exact measure, record fifteen minutes of finished narration and then check your manuscript. Did you narrate been 2,000 and 2,500 words (8–10,000 per hour)? You did? You're all set.

7

Intro to Engineering

Rethinking

ENGINEERING, or post-recording processing, is typically broken down into four major elements:

- Completed recording
- "The Listen"
- Processing
- Proofing

The Listen is listening to the entire file and fixing every error. This is far and away the longest and hardest task of the entire process. It involves removing every click, checking for missed words, incorrect voicing, and many other elements we'll look at in a later chapter.

Once that is done, then there is the Processing. This is the step in which the recording is tweaked electronically to achieve the best possible sound result. This step can be very complex to set up. However, once it is set up, it is then very easy to run.

The Proofing is a second listen to make sure that the audiobook is as clean as possible and that the engineer didn't make any mistakes as they manipulated the manuscript. This is especially important to make sure that the Processing step—which can be highly automated once it is set up properly—didn't damage the file in some unpredictable way.

So, I spent some time rethinking these steps.

Keeping It Clean

This is where "recording clean" that I mentioned earlier really pays off. By making the original recording completely or nearly completely accurate, it's possible to literally halve the post-recording process effort.

Why is this? It has to do with "pickups." A pickup is a re-record to fix a narration mistake that is beyond the capability of the engineer to fix—mispronunciation, garbled words, frog in the throat, and so on, as mentioned earlier.

If one starts with a clean and accurate-as-possible recording, then it's possible to reorganize the post-recording process. In fact, I would suggest that every inaccuracy allowed to escape the recording process also degrades the finished result due to voice and emotional variations in the pickup narration.

The rethinking of the process below only works if you start with a clean recording.

By breaking apart the process and reorganizing the

process, I was able to vastly accelerate the entire sequence and entirely remove one of the slower steps.

Here's my revised process:

- End of recording check
- Processing
- The Listen

By the time The Listen task is complete, the "Proof Listen" will also be done—entirely removing that long, slow step of critically listening to the entire book again. (When I trained my assistant to be my engineer, I *did* do proof listening until I was comfortable with her consistency.)

Some More Detail

Recording

- Once done recording, review the file for overlarge spikes (they stand out clearly as we'll see in a moment). Fix these immediately as part of the recording process or re-record if necessary.
- When the recording is complete and de-spiked, save a "safe" copy of the file in case something goes wrong.

Engineering

- Run a Click Remover to remove the bulk of extraneous clicks.

- Run a set of pre-defined effects (yes, we'll study these in detail) to complete the processing cleanup.
- Run two more automated steps (that are typically run last).
- Run a validation check that the file will meet the required export criteria.

At this point, we have taken 1–5 minutes (depending on the file size and your computer's speed) to prove that the recording is valid for uploading to the distributors. If it isn't, we have very little time invested so far. We've also removed a vast majority of the audio problems that would normally have to be hand corrected. (*This* is why to use Adobe Audition.)

THE LISTEN

- Complete the Metadata fields.
- Do The Listen.
- My assistant returns the finished product to me, with a set of notes of things she was unable to fix. I'm able to fix almost all of them without re-recording. I then teach her those advanced techniques and she gains that skill, giving me less to do next time. (Now, almost every one of her notes are things that are wholly acceptable but she wants my stamp of approval, as it's my audiobook after all.)
- I save the file in the proper format (since I'm already in the file to review her notes).
- She uploads them to all of the vendors.

To repeat: there is one major disadvantage to this process.

If I need to re-record a word or section, it can be tricky to match the sound. Why? Because I must re-record the patch. Then, rather than listening to see if it fits, I must fully process the patch (which takes less than a minute but includes a number of steps) and then I can paste it into the master file. If I listen and it doesn't fit smoothly, I can try to tweak it or, once again I re-record, process, and patch until I'm satisfied with the resulting sound.

For the trade-off of removing the entire proof listen and decreasing the number of fixes required by my assistant (which used to be done by me) by over 75%, I'm glad to make that trade-off.

Saving and Naming Conventions

I save files at every step:

- Raw = recording complete
- Post Process = automated processing done (once comfortable with it, you may skip saving this step)
- Post Listen = the engineering process is complete except for notes back to the reader / proof listen if to be done
- Final WAV = final uncompressed master file (keep this forever)
- Final MP3 = compressed file ready to upload

HERE ARE TYPICAL NAMING EXAMPLES:

- CH00-Title-Front Matter-raw.wav
- CH01-Title-Post Process.wav
- CH02-Title-Post Listen.wav
- CH98-Title-Back Matter-final.wav
- CH99-Title-sample.mp3

End of Recording Check - The Spikes

The main thing that needs to be checked for at the end of the recording is bad spikes. No matter how careful you are, you won't catch all of these while recording. These take two forms: fixable and not.

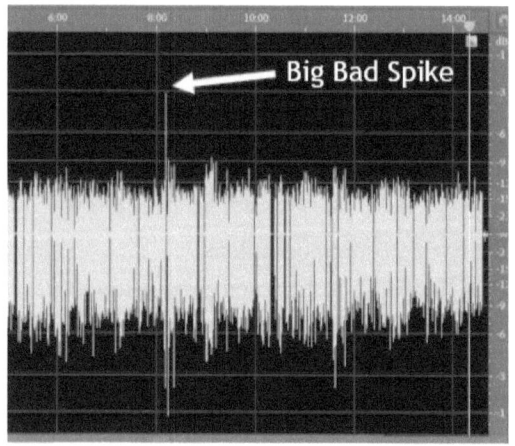

If the spike doesn't hit the 0 dB limits that are typically the top and bottom edges of your view window, it is probably fixable. If it exceeds these, it must be re-recorded.

Tip: Because you haven't applied any effects or done any engineering yet, nothing special needs to be done to re-record a section. Simply highlight the problem area, press record, and go. (Remember, almost all tools have an undo tool if you mess up something—Cmd or Cntrl Z.)

There are two ways in Audition to deal with probably-fixable spikes.

Turn It Down

If you zoom in on the spike (+ key or mouse scroll up), you will soon be able to isolate the second that was recorded too loudly. Listen to see if it was simply too loud or if there an annoying pop or some other unwanted sound that must be recorded over.

If it's simply too loud (perhaps you leaned closer to the mike for a moment), you can highlight the section (do it from a silent moment to a silent moment, typically from one breath or phrase to the next) and a small volume knob will appear. Dial it down until the spike is of similar size to the sounds around it.

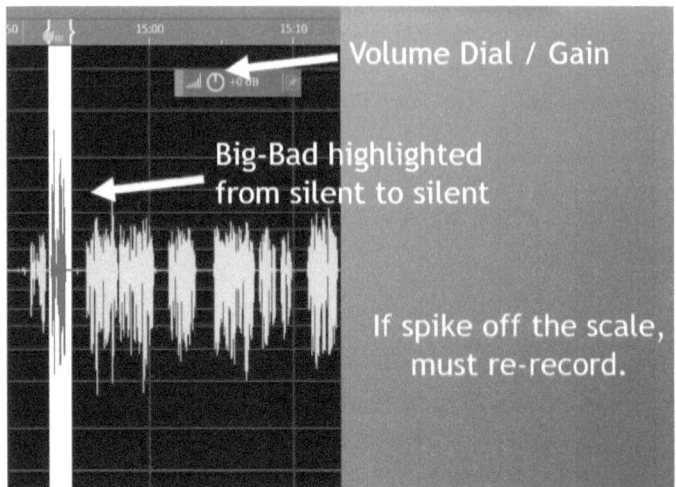

Done!

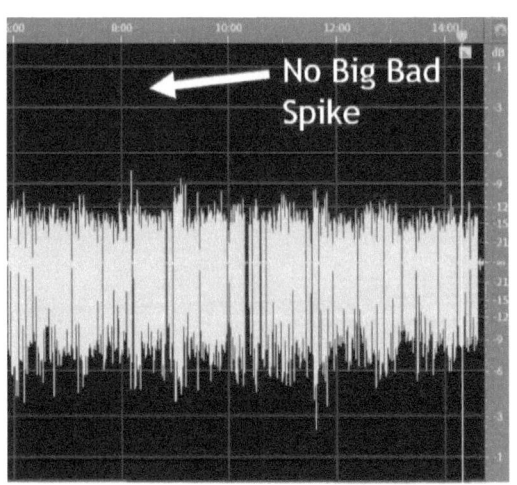

Rub It Out

If it is a sharp tick or pop that can't be isolated and deleted, if may be possible to "heal" the problem with an Audition Bandage tool. Select the Spectrum Window from the menu, then the bandage tool, which looks like a Band-Aid.

Setting the size of the eraser, you can actually see the unwanted spike as a hot, yellow color. Rub the bandage cursor over the spike. It will probably clear it right off. Be careful to not erase more sound than you intended. (Remember the Undo History tool.)

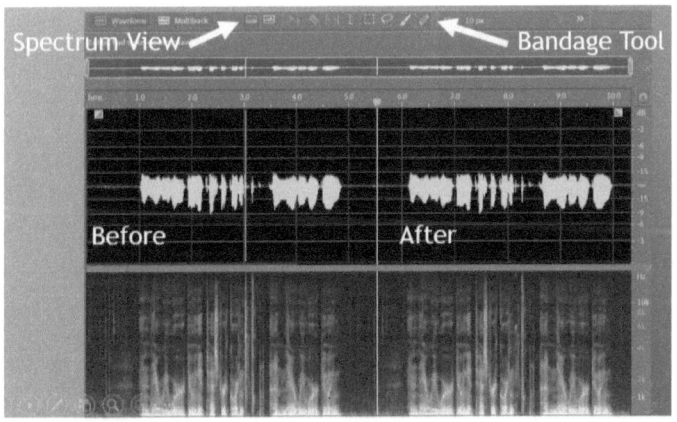

TRIM IT

Sometimes, on a particularly narrow spike, you can zoom in, highlight just the spike if it's narrow enough, and tap the delete key. (You'll want to highlight it from where it crosses the middle "silence" line to where it crosses the line while going in the same direction. If it's a rising curve, soaring upward, you'll want to go to the next place after the spike where it crosses upward.)

These spikes must be fixed prior to engineering, especially if you are sending them out to a professional engineer.

8

Engineering

JUST A HEADS UP, this is the techy, geeky chapter. This is the only chapter like this—and the only one necessary—where we will discuss detailed tools and settings. If it seems overwhelming to read, then think of it instead as a step-by-step guide to setting up Adobe Audition properly for use.

Again, if you opted to use a different DAW software, you'll have to adapt what you do to that software's capability.

If you choose to outsource your engineering, then you don't really need this chapter. Though I do recommend reading through it at least once as we will also talk about some principles of sound itself. These will be useful when talking with your engineer.

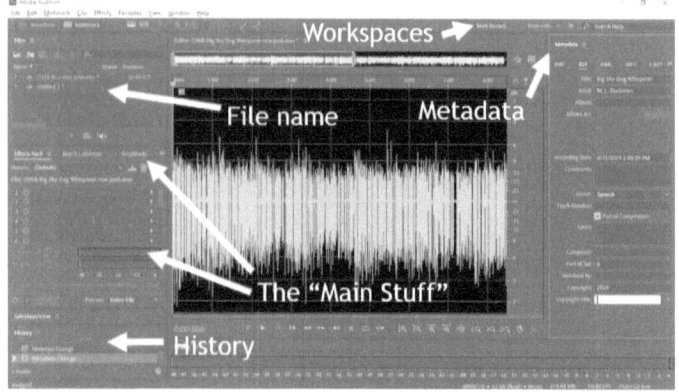

Audition Workspaces

Adobe Audition (in the upper right corner) has the ability to set and save workspaces. A workspace is what shows or doesn't show on the screen.

For recording, I hide almost all of the windows. All I have showing is Window / Editor and Window / Level meters. I call the workspace "Matt-record."

When I am editing, I change to a separate, pre-saved workspace that I wildly call "Matt-edit." This workspace adds on: Amplitude Statistics, Files, History, Metadata, Selection/View, and Tools.

Once set up, it's a single mouse click to switch between the two screen layouts.

What follows below is a step-by-step explanation of every step I use to clean, process, and test audio. Are there other methods possible? There are over sixty effects (pre-loaded—you can get many more), each with numerous settings that can be used singly or in combination to correct and alter sound. Even the order these effects are used in can drastically alter the results.

Here's the roadmap I've come up with for myself and it should work fine for any audiobook narration with only minor adjustments:

- Automatic Click Remover
- DeHummer
- Dynamic Processing
- DeEsser
- Graphic Equalizer (20-Band)
- Single-Band Compressor

Then, once the effects are completed (they only need to be set up once, then they run very quickly as a saved group), there are three more steps:

- Match Loudness – Total RMS
- Match Loudness – Peak Amplitude
- Amplitude Statistics

A pretty scary looking list. However, they are each very straightforward and will hopefully be easy and clear to use by the end of this chapter.

Automatic Click Remover

Effect > Noise Reduction / Restoration > Automatic Click Remover

This does exactly what it says: it removes a large number of unwanted clicks. The tool must be used with some care, as it can also remove all of the higher tones from your voice.

Rack Effect - Automatic Click Remover

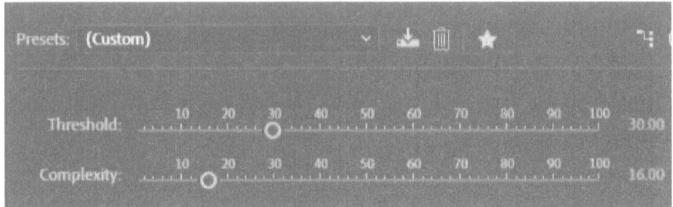

Settings:

- Threshold = 30
- Complexity = 15

How did I come up with these settings? I highlighted a short section of audio. Then I selected the Automatic Click Remover Effect. By clicking on the auto-replay (which looks like a looping rectangle with a small arrow in it), then clicking on the play arrow, I can listen to how it is changing the sound as I fiddle with the settings. I can even select and deselect the green power button that controls whether or not the effect is engaged as I listen.

Now, by moving the sliders side to side, I will listen for the highest numeric settings I can but still detect no changes to the actual voice. It may remove clicks, but you don't want it affecting your voice.

Effects Rack

An Effects Rack is the way Adobe Audition saves a preset effect or group of effects. This allows us to set it up one time and then apply them later with a single click when we want to.

Tip: Like all programs, Adobe Audition has the ability to crowd too many options into a small window in order to conserve desktop space. If your workstation is set up like mine, there will be a little slider of options in the middle of the left side that include: Effects Rack, Match Loudness, Amplitude Statistics, and Properties. But you won't be able to see them all at once. Click on the double arrows << or >> to find these options and then click on them to change your view.

DeHummer

Effects > Noise Reduction > DeHummer

Hum (also called Line Hum) is typically caused by microphones picking up the hum noise of your wall's electrical current (think a very low, steady *mmmmmmm*). Most modern equipment is well-enough designed to be isolated from line hum now and it shouldn't be an issue. But it isn't a bad practice to filter for this anyway.

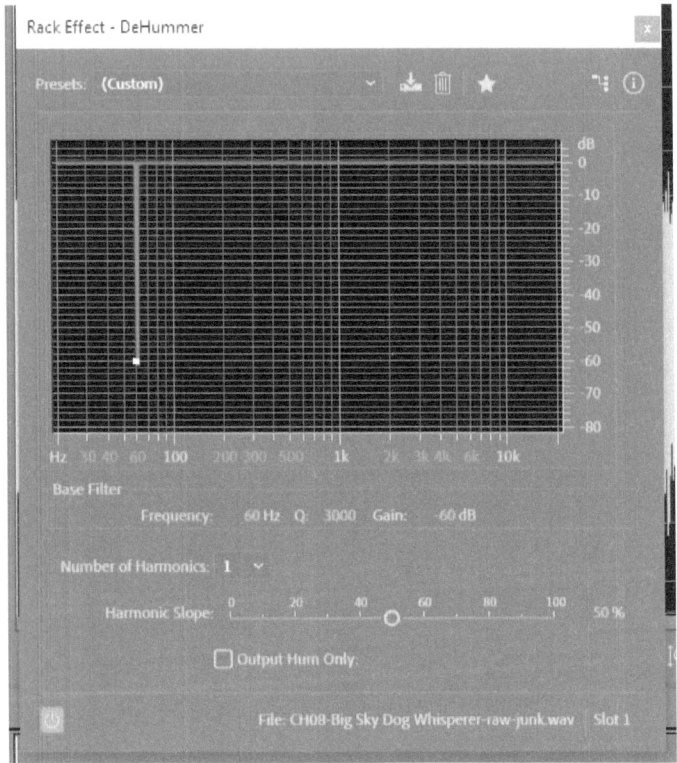

- Frequency = 60 Hz (50 Hz in most places outside of North America and parts of South America)
- Q = 3,000
- Gain = -60 dB (this means take anything at 60 Hz and turn it down by 60 decibels, which is a lot)
- Number of Harmonics = 1 (unless you have a

real problem, then try 2 or 3 but watch out for a bad ringing tone to the result, 1 is best)
- Harmonic slope = 50%

If you still have a problem, try plugging the amplifier power cord (if you have one) into a different outlet, or flipping it over. Often, plugging into a power strip (which is good practice anyway) will solve this. It may also be a sign of a bad microphone cable, which is quite inexpensive to replace.

Dynamics Processing

Effects > Amplitude and Compression > Dynamics Processing

This is an incredibly powerful tool and it alone is worth the price of Audition. It can save hours (literally) on the engineering process. It may seem a little confusing at first, but if you stick with it, you'll have command of one of the most powerful tools there is.

Rack Effect - Dynamics Processing

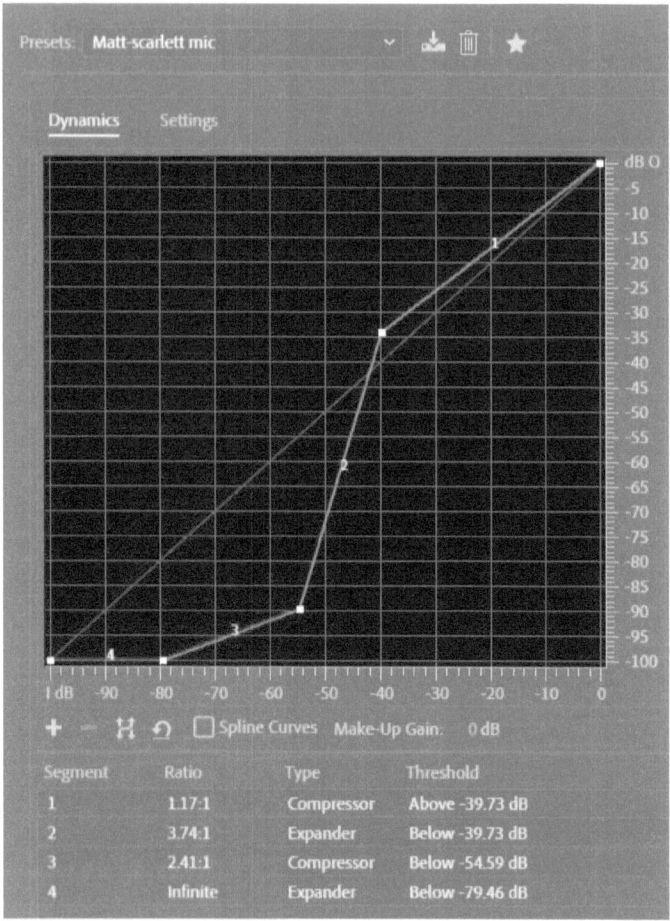

When you first open it, there will be a straight line running diagonally across the graph from lower left to upper right. The way to read it is: "If a sound is this loud across the bottom (x-axis), then I want it to be this loud up the side (y-axis)."

In other words, it can make soft sounds, such as breaths and distant car noise, softer. And, at the same time, it can make stronger sounds (such as your narration voice) louder).

Caution: Like most audio tools, it is very easy to distort a voice badly. However, the settings here should work well.

- Leave the two end points at their corners.
- Click on the + sign to create a draggable point on the line, and then use your mouse to approximate these settings.
- Set one point where the grid lines meet for -80 along the bottom lines up with -100 along the side. ("If a sound is -80 dB in strength, make it 20 dB quieter." In other words, just make it go away.)
- Set a second point where the grid lines meet for -45 on the bottom and -80 along the side. ("Suppress but don't quash smaller breaths.")
- Third point: -40 dB on the bottom to -35 dB on the top. ("Slightly strengthen the softer part of the stuff we want, the voice.")0

I wouldn't make a stronger change than this upward because it can create unwanted echo sounds. Especially, don't try to fully suppress the background noises such as your breathing. We'll discuss why during "The Listen" chapter.

DeEsser

Effects > Amplitude and Compression > DeEsser

Just as the name says, this tool can fix overly sibilant S sounds.

Rack Effect - DeEsser

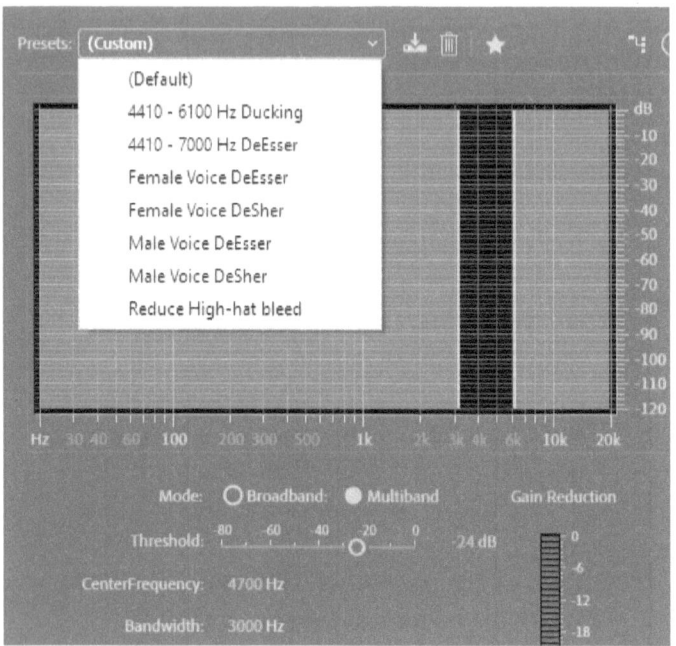

Like most of the effects, there is a variety of pre-built settings that may be found by clicking on the down arrow for "Presets." This tool offers male and female DeEssers and male and female DeShers. If you over-aspirate your *sh* sounds, then you may want to add this effect to your rack twice—once for the *s* and once for the *sh* correction.

A good rule of thumb in all audio is: the less you do to the sound, the better. So I use the preset as a starting point and I then, with audio looping as noted in the Automatic Click Remover discussion above, try to decrease the settings to the least change possible while still fixing the *s* or *sh* problem.

- Multiband.

- Drag the two white verticals as close together as possible to still fix the sound.
- Then slide the Threshold as far to the right as possible (-25 dB worked well for me).

Graphic Equalizer (20-band)

Effects > Filter and EQ > Graphic Equalizer (20-band)

This is another very powerful tool and should be used with caution. This is also the tool that you will probably spend the most time getting set correctly.

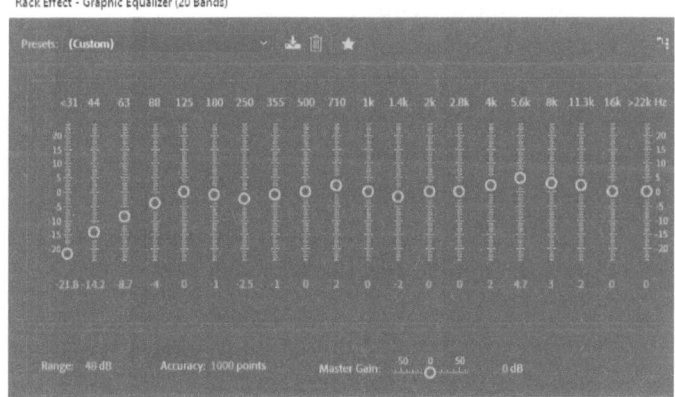

It is very simple in concept. There are 20 sliders, each affecting a narrow range of frequency from very low at the left to very high at the right. You may safely ignore everything on the screen except the sliders themselves and the number directly below each slider. The last two at either end affect things like bass drums and sizzling cymbals. Our issues lie in the middle ground.

Tip: The 10-band EQ doesn't offer enough control

and the 30-band is overkill. Twenty sliders are plenty for the task of an audiobook.

Rules of thumb:

- Think in small changes. If you are shifting a slider by more than +/- 5 dB (shown directly beneath each slider), you are probably making too drastic a change.
- Think in curves. If you want to adjust a slider by +5 dB, set the ones to either side at +3 dB and the next set out at +1 dB.
- Most of the human voice falls between 200 Hz (low male) and 800 Hz (high female). However, the human voice is very rich in harmonics and overtones, which will extend that range upward as high as 4,000 Hz (or 4 kHz). What this means is that you will typically be adjusting only the middle 10 sliders for your voice range.

This is also the tool that is used for making adjustments for the sounds of your recording space.

- If the room is "too well" deadened, you may want to add in some higher settings in the 4–12 kHz range to increase the brightness or liveliness of the recording. Caution: this can also increase the noise level drastically, so do this very sparingly and leave those far-right sliders mostly alone.
- If the room is a little reverberant, try easing off on the lower tones below 250 Hz.
- Personally, I have a very deep voice that can

overwhelm the balance of the higher tones. So, I slightly decrease the lower end to ease back on the power of my chest voice.
- Then I roll off the very low end because it reduces incidental rumble and, as I'm not playing a bass guitar, I don't need it anyway.

Tips:

- Remember that part about "Getting over your own voice?" This is where it matters. Listen to it over and over until it no longer feels like your voice. Not by over-adjusting it, but rather by breaking it down into component parts as you listen. Is the high end a little too high, making it sound brassy? Is the low too light, making the recorded voice sound thin? Don't think of it as *your* voice; think of it as *a* voice that it is now your task to make sound as awesome as possible.
- Don't go for brassy. Podcast and radio voices are often overly bright and we've become used to that. It's not a comfortable sound for audiobooks.

Single-band Compressor

Effects > Amplitude and Compression > Single-band Compressor

Rack Effect - Single-band Compressor

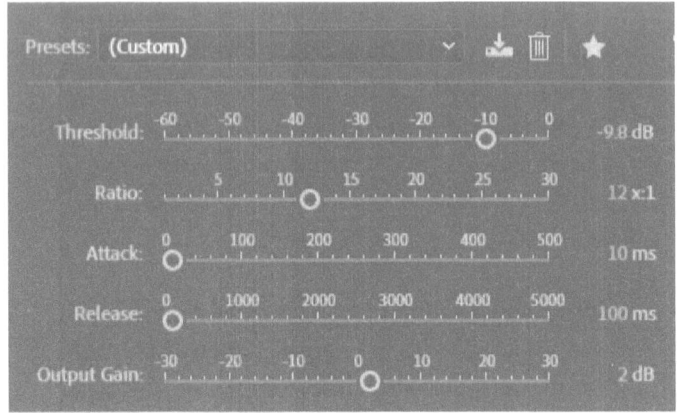

This effect is a wondrous tool that evens out wide volume variations. Not the drastic peaks, but perhaps where your energy fell during the middle of the chapter, it rebalances the volumes.

Think of it as fixing that problem with the movie you're watching on TV. The dialog is too soft, then the thrilling scene roars out at you. It's because the compression was set for movie theater dynamics and never readjusted for listening on your home TV.

This tool can just as easily break your recording as make it. These settings have served me well:

- Threshold = -25
- Ratio = 2.4
- Attack = 0
- Release = 0
- Output Gain = 2 dB

Tip: Use the final output gain to adjust the finished

volume of your recording for the overall Effects Rack. If you notice that running the Effects Rack "squishes" your audio (makes it softer), compensate by using the Output Gain to make it louder. If the final result expands particularly, use the Output Gain to soften it.

Summary of Effects Rack

Once all this is set up and saved in your "Effects Rack Presets," it is a very simple process for every recording in the future:

- Open the file.
- Select your pre-saved Effects Rack.
- Select "Entire File" in Process (it should already say this).
- Click Apply.

Now you're ready for the last 3 steps and they are very easy.

This is a good time to save your file just in case.

Match Loudness - Total RMS

You really don't care about the meaning of the Total Root Mean Square volume of the file. What you care about is setting your target volume to -18 dB, then clicking Run.

We may have to come back and run it at -17 dB, but we'll get to that.

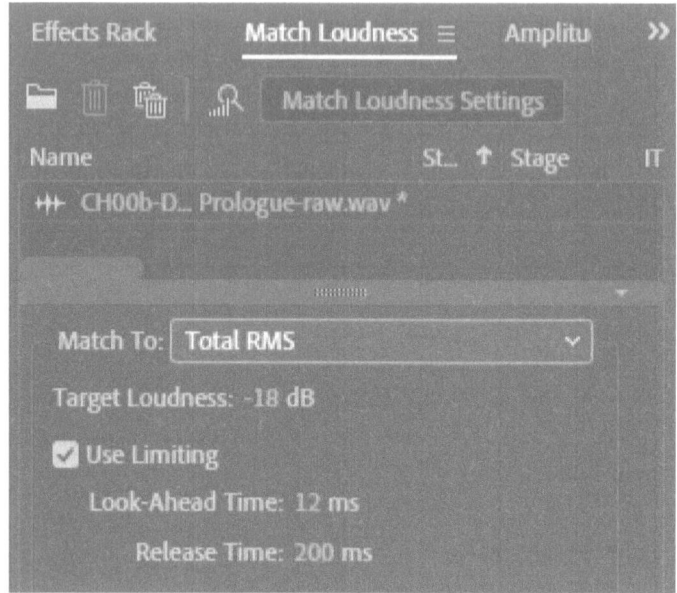

Match Loudness - Peak Amplitude

Again, we don't care what it means (how loud is the loudest sound in the file). We just set it to -3.5 dB and click run.

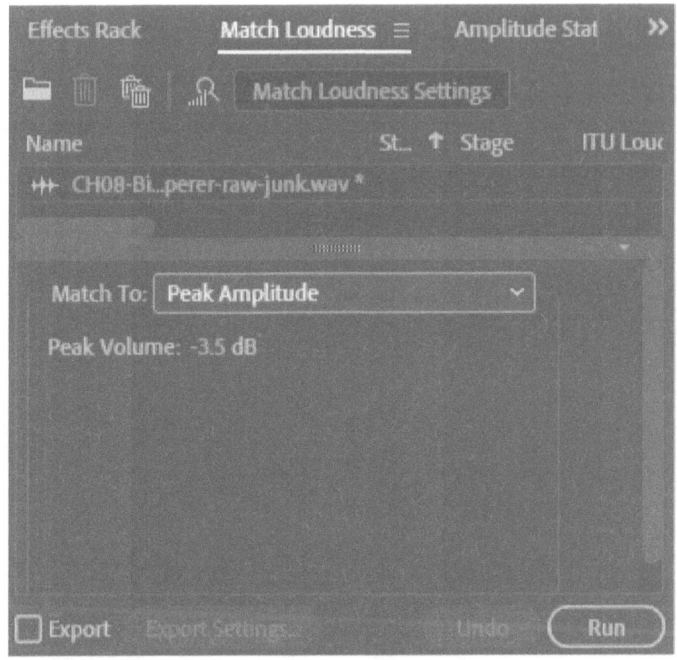

Amplitude Statistics

Click Run.

The Total RMS Amplitude *MUST* be between -18 dB and -23 dB or your file will be rejected by the vendors. (This is the only number here that you care about.)

The primary fix if you end up above -18 dB is to back up two steps (or close the file without saving and reopen the saved file), then Match Loudness – Total RMS at -17 (or -19) dB.

Metadata

On the right side of your screen, if it's laid out like my illustrations, is the Metadata window. This is how your file will be electronically cataloged. There are three critical fields and two optional ones that it's hard to tell what their effect is, but I fill out anyway.

- Title (the book)
- Artist (you)
- Genre = speech (optional)
- Part of set (Chapter # - I use 0 for intro material)
- Copyright year

The Final Tweaks

There is one very simple task to make an audiobook listenable—well-place silence. There is some variability allowed, but these are "best numbers."

- 0.5 seconds before any audio starts in the file (such as chapter number).
- 2.5 seconds between chapter title / number / subtitle and the first word of the text.
- 3.5–4.0 seconds at the end of each file.
- Personally, I leave 3.5–4.0 seconds for scene breaks.

Save this file!

This is a critical save point. Your next task will take several hours per finished hour and will prove very frustrating if you have to throw it away and start over. Don't make matters worse by having to re-process the file as well.

9

The Listen

THE LISTEN IS the big kahuna of the audiobook post-recording process. It takes the most time and the most finesse. This step can literally make or break an audiobook's success.

The purpose of The Listen is manifold: listening for a wide variety of errors, fixing them, and improving the overall delivery of the narrator's voice. These engineering skills will grow over time just as assuredly as narration skills will.

However, don't worry about any lack of skill in the beginning. Once we've walked through the steps of The Listen in this chapter, you will be creating a high-quality product—it will only keep getting better after that.

Stamina

Just like recording, The Listen requires a lot of concentration—something that lags with time and weariness. For this reason, I only rarely record in sessions longer than two hours. The same is true for this step. Multiple, shorter sessions are the best practice.

Take a break every hour (good advice anyway). Take a short walk, make some tea, listen to music—anything to clear your head so that you can refocus on the task at hand. I schedule this kind of work across several days for a title rather than trying to lump it all together. Perhaps write in the morning, then record. The next day, write in the morning, then engineer.

How professionals do this for an eight-hour day, I have no idea.

Setup

- Get comfortable, this is going to take a while.
- Wear good headphones. Speakers simply don't cut it. And not earbuds. You need good quality, over-the-ear headphones (the ones that look like earmuffs) to hear the finest details.
- Listen a little more loudly than is comfortable. This means that you will be hearing more detail than almost all listeners. If you fix anything that *you* can hear, then they certainly won't notice it at the lower volume settings.
- Have a copy of the manuscript in front of you. You will want to follow along as you listen to watch for missed or incorrect words and incorrect voicing.

Tip: Recording an audiobook is an exceptional way to do a final proofread of your book. After the editor, copyeditor, and proofreader are done, there may still be stray mistakes. Reading the entire book aloud is a great way to find them.

Recording Errors

These are errors that you missed in your narration.

- *Missed words.* It is surprisingly easy to skip a word. I have a real problem as a narrator with –*n't* endings. Can versus can't nearly made me insane early on. I caught those errors during The Listen.
- *Garbled words.* "Clive turned to the peesher and shot him with a sleep dart." You mangled the "preacher" without noticing.
- *Mispronounced words.* We touched on this earlier. For the life of me, I can't say "cockpit" while recording, it always comes out "cotpit"…and I write a lot of airborne military tales. I'm always having to go find a good *k* sound and insert that in after the fact.
- *Stressed the wrong syllable.* Especially in foreign words. Even if you got the sounds right, where *is* the stress on the syllable?
- *Wrong voice.* In our earlier example, Stan has a big, deep voice. He's in an argument with Jodie, who has a middle-high voice. Suddenly I slip up and Jodie speaks a line in a big deep voice.

Here're ways to fix these:

- *Missed words.* I like to keep an electronic copy of

the book open in the background while I'm doing The Listen. A quick search can reveal if I used that word somewhere else, preferably in the same voice. With a little care and hunting, I can copy that word and insert the missing sound.
- *Garbled words.* These can be fixed with the same technique. It may also be possible to clip out an extraneous sound, such as a third L that shouldn't be there.
- *Mispronounced words.* Again, manually search and replace to fix the wrong segment. Though you may need to re-record to resolve this particular error.
- *Stressed wrong syllable.* This can be surprisingly easy to fix. Highlight the over-stressed syllable and use the volume dial to turn it down a bit. Then highlight the under-stressed syllable and turn it up a bit. Works almost every time.
- *Wrong Voice.* This one is fun. Open up our old friend the Graphic Equalizer (20-band). Did you record the voice too low? Roll out some of the bass tones and increase some of the high ones. Vice versa if you recorded it too high. Remember to think in small adjustments and with slow curves in the sliders to either side to maintain an authentic sound. This technique takes a bit of practice but works wonders. There is an effect designed specifically to alter pitch, but I've never had much luck with it. Too many options, too fussy. Stick with the EQ if you can.

Technical Errors

These are the stray sounds.

- Clicks (typically mouth noise—you didn't eat dairy before recording did you?)
- For a while I had a high squeak deep in my throat until I learn how to open my mouth wider. Now it only comes back if the lilacs are blooming (to which I'm quite allergic). I take a pill and I'm fine.
- Rumble of a passing truck or motorcycle that you didn't account for.

All of these can typically be cured by judicious use of the volume control, snipping out a section, or practicing with the Bandage tool in the Spectrum view. The last is particularly useful if there is heavy vehicle noise, as it tends to be very low. Try rubbing the Bandage tool across the lowest portion of the spectrum view. You can remove a great deal of rumble without much affecting the voice.

Clean Up Breathing

Specifically, cleaning up the narrator's breathing.

I'm referring to the *sound* of the narrator's breath. A common beginning engineering mistake is to "flatten" out all breathing sounds—turn each breath gap to absolute silence. This actually creates an unnatural sounding recording and will be disturbing to the audio listener for reasons they can't determine. At most they'll say that it sounds uncomfortable. At worst, they'll stop listening.

Most of the breath sounds have been softened by the

settings we established in Dynamics Processing in Chapter 8. But they haven't been removed.

Now, as part of The Listen, you want to listen for overly loud breaths. Simply highlight them and turn down the volume knob—typically -30 dB should be plenty unless it is a particularly egregious one.

If you find yourself doing this a lot, you're either over-correcting or your microphone is too close to a direct line to your mouth. If you've chosen my inverted microphone technique, perhaps you're tipping your head up to talk *to* the microphone. Don't. The whole point of that arrangement is to get the microphone out of your breathing path.

Another common mistake is to remove the duration of the breath rather than the volume of the breath. With no gaps, the listener won't be able to tolerate listening for very long. The reason is that, for the most part, the listener breathes at the same time as the narrator. Providing the listener with no place to breathe will make them feel very anxious.

Clean Up Pacing

This is an advanced technique.

Once you are skilled at listening for recording errors, technical errors, and proper breaths, it's time to look at the next level up.

Ideally, a read-by-author narration will have the exact pacing that the author / narrator intended. However, as we've seen, the recording booth is a very busy place. As a narrator you will be distracted by technical issues and stray thoughts. ("I could have written that dialog better.") You may be running short of breath and take an overlong time to gather some air. I slow distinctly when I'm making sure that I pronounce an unfamiliar word or name correctly. Also, perhaps you hurried a transition.

Inserting and removing portions of silence are very simple tasks: highlight and copy / paste or delete sections of the nearly-flat breath gaps. Use this technique judiciously and don't spend too much time doing it. The more you second guess yourself, the more time you'll spend and the higher your chance of damaging the final result.

Pickups

Pickups are the industry phrase for the re-recording needed from the narrator. These are necessary for anything that you were unable to fix during The Listen. The goal is to minimize pickups as much as possible.

If you expend even a few minutes of extra time in the recording booth, it is practical to nearly eliminate the necessity of a pickup.

With practice of advanced skill levels with the techniques in Chapter 8, Engineering, it is possible to wholly eliminate them. I haven't done a single pickup in my last five titles. However, that's after twenty-five titles of practice. Don't expect to achieve this right away.

Now be sure to SAVE YOUR FILE, preferably with a suffix of "Final" to make sure you don't mix it up with any uncorrected files.

The Listen Summary

The Listen is a matter of balance.

Too little attention to detail will create a sloppy product that will be off-putting to listeners.

Too much attention can add hours to the process for little actual improvement in the overall product.

Remember that the read-by-author space is a forgiving one. Listeners expect less *perfection* in these finished results, but this isn't a podcast or webinar. This is an audiobook and listeners expect a certain quality.

I have a friend who wants to just sit by a microphone and read his books. If he messes up, he intends to just say "Sorry" and reread the section without removing the mistake and with no further editing. Every time he brings this up, every audiobook listener in the room shouts him down.

There is still a standard that's expected by audiobook listeners.

What is it?

They don't want to be bumped out of the story. They want to lose themselves in the story, in your story. Listeners should never have quality issues force them to be aware that they're listening to an audiobook. You only want them to hear your words. That should be your standard.

10

Final Steps

Sample

NOW THAT YOU'VE completed the recording and engineering of your files, you need to create a sample file for vendors to post.

It is:

- Less than 5 minutes long.
- Typically the first 2–5 minutes of your first chapter.
- Recorded without the chapter number. If your chapters are named, you might choose to include that.
- You want the end of the sample to be on some sort of cliffhanger that will make the listener want to go out and purchase your book right away to keep listening. If that moment is thirty seconds into your first chapter, stop there. If it's 5:30 into your first chapter, consider cutting a

paragraph or two out of the middle of the sample to get there in under 5 minutes.
- After first saving a new copy of your entire Chapter 1 to a "Sample" file (you don't want to risk losing all that work), save and trim off the chapter number and everything past your cliffhanger. (Remember to add 0.5 seconds of silence at the front of the file and 3–4 seconds at the end.)
- Save the file with the name "Sample."

Saving Your Files

Saving your files properly for sale is a relatively easy task, but it must be done correctly, or the distributors will reject your audiobook files.

There are two file types we are concerned with in audiobook narration.

- A WAV file (pronounced "wave"). This is an uncompressed raw file. What that means is that every nuance of your recording is preserved in these large files. They are acoustically the best. However, they are also prohibitively large.
- An MP3 (pronounced "M-P-three") is a compressed audio file. This compression will be of very high quality if done properly, but it will not have all of the audio information. In order to save space (they're roughly one-eighth the size of a WAV file), a great deal of information is interpreted, compacted, or even shaved. The result is still very listenable, especially for something as simple as a recorded voice. But it will not have the studio

level quality of a WAV file. Because of the convenience, the MP3 is the standard file of a downloadable audiobook. (All of your music downloads are MP3 or a closely related compressed file type.)

Until this time, we've been working with WAV files (in Audition). Here are the simple steps, after you save the final WAV, to properly create and save an MP3 file.

OPEN FILE > SAVE AS

- Select Format: MP3
- Select Sample Type: Change button

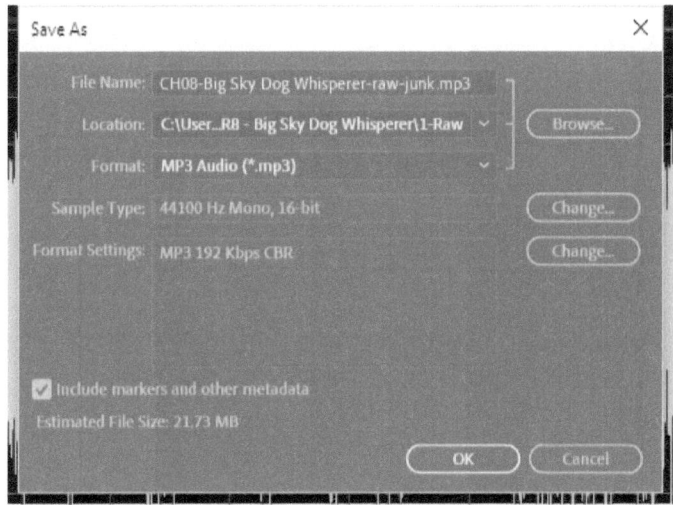

CONVERT SAMPLE TYPE

You can set up the criteria on this screen once and then save it as a preset:

- Sample Rate: 44,100
- Quality: 100%
- Channels: Mono (unless you are doing complex, full-cast audio and have studied the proper use of multi-channel mixing to stereo, you want mono)
- Bit Depth: 16

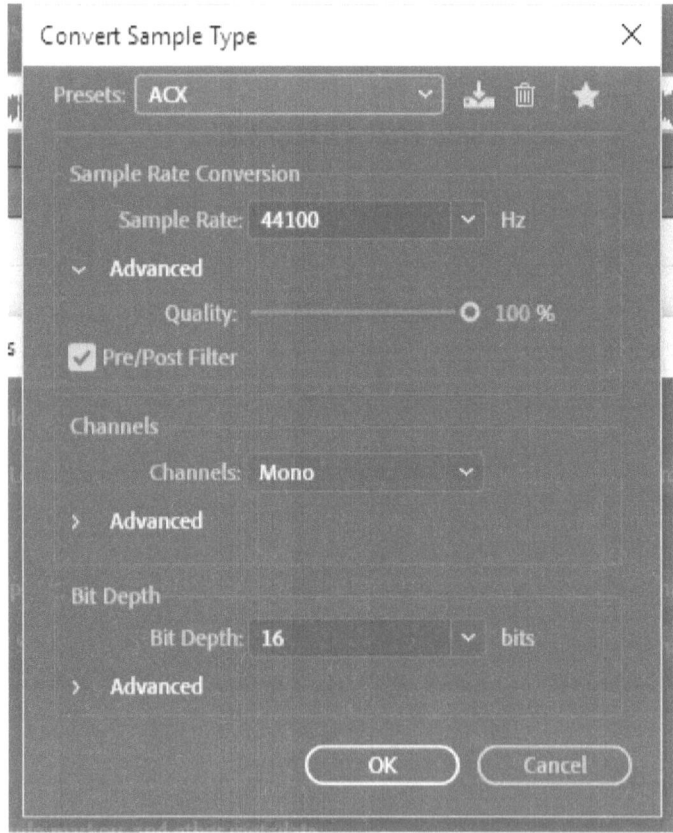

Save

Costs

One of the biggest considerations of audiobooks is production costs.

If this book has shown anything, it has shown that it is not a simple or fast process. However, I hope that it has also shown that it is eminently possible to record your own high-quality audiobook with very low capital cost.

The thing you must assess for yourself is the indirect costs. An indirect cost is something that doesn't cost you money but can impact you in other ways. In this case, the trade-off is time.

What value do you place on your time?

This is not a book on the subject (as there are already many fine sites and books on this topic), but you must consider the cost of your time.

- To record your first minute of audio will probably take several hours to set up.
- To record a full hour could well take you 2–3 hours in the beginning, though I have been able to squeeze that down to 1:20 per hour with practice.
- To engineer your first minute of audio could take 5–10 hours to set up, if you follow the steps in this book. My first minute took me closer to fifty hours but that included a lot of learning what didn't work.
- To engineer an hour of finished audio (including The Listen) could take 4–5 hours

early on. We have it down to 2 hours (again, you should get there more quickly with the information in this guide).

That is all a substantial time investment that could be spent writing and creating new items for sale.

Personally, I think it is worth it because of the rapidly growing popularity of audiobooks. I like having an additional product to sell for each book I write: e-book, print, and audio.

But you must determine what's best for you and for your business.

Distribution

In the time it took me to type this sentence, something has probably changed in the audiobook distribution and marketing world. It is evolving that quickly.

Twelve months ago, the only practical way to sell your read-by-author audiobooks was by loading them to ACX. From there it was distributed to Amazon, Apple iTunes, and Audible. There was an obscure company called Author's Republic that could reach several markets, but it meant taking much less royalty than from ACX (at the time you had to go exclusively to ACX or exclusively to Author's Republic).

In the last twelve months:

- Findaway Voices opened up a channel for author-produced audiobooks.
- Apple broke the ACX choke hold and is now accepting titles from Findaway Voices and other vendors.

- Kobo is testing a direct channel and I suspect Apple isn't far behind.
- Storytel is a Swedish company that is making audio-first release a new standard in Scandinavia.
- Library lending is coming online fast.
- This is all aside from direct sales off your website, presently facilitated by Findaway Voices' Authors Direct program.
- Many countries are plunging into audiobooks, even English-language audiobooks, because the non-English speakers wish to learn better English.

Did I mention that this market is changing quickly?

Personally, I'm a big fan of a broad distribution base; I don't like having all of my eggs in one basket. I currently load to ACX (non-exclusive), Findaway Voices through Draft2Digital, and a couple of beta-test programs that will probably be public by the time this book is published six weeks from now.

Talk to other authors. Stay current.

One Launch or Two

This is a very common question: "Should I launch my audiobook with my e-book and print versions? Or should I launch it later as a marketing campaign to refresh the title?"

Simultaneous launch takes a fair amount of planning.

- Once you finish writing the book and get it back from the copyeditor and then the proofreader, it is finally ready to record.

- The recording process, depending upon your speed and available time, can take several weeks. If you are outsourcing the engineering, they have a lead time as well.
- Most audio vendors require at least three weeks to clear an audiobook through their process and then publish it.
- Most vendors don't have pre-orders available for audiobooks yet. But, once you have completed audiobook files, you can e-mail them and request a pre-order to be set up. Or a fixed release date.

I'm not saying it isn't doable, I'm just saying that you need to plan at least two months of time between when the proofreader is finished with a title and the title goes on sale for the best sales results.

However, all evidence points to a far greater sales rate for simultaneous release than a staggered launch. If you can pull it off, it's worth it.

As of July 1, 2019, it is my tiny company's policy to never again launch a novel without simultaneous audio. We'll see how that goes.

Final Tips

Stand up when recording.

Keep your energy high. (Not annoyingly bubbly, but high and focused.)

Have fun! (Because not only can your listener tell but, if you aren't, what's the point?)

Other titles in the Strategies for Success series

Managing Your Inner Artist / Writer

Explore the working relationship every artist must cultivate between the artistic self and their business self.

Estate Planning for Authors

Your Final Letter and why you need to write it now

A practical guide to organizing your intellectual property and preparing your chosen heirs to ensure that your writing and your income continue to benefit them out to the limits of copyright.

Character Voice

Creating Unique and Memorable Characters

Tools, tools, and more tools on how to create distinct voices for your characters.

Available at fine retailers everywhere

About the Author

M.L. "Matt" Buchman started the first of over 60 novels, 100 short stories, and a fast-growing pile of audiobooks while flying from South Korea to ride his bicycle across the Australian Outback. Part of a solo around the world trip that ultimately launched his writing career in: thrillers, military romantic suspense, contemporary romance, and SF/F.

Recently named in *The 20 Best Romantic Suspense Novels: Modern Masterpieces* by ALA's Booklist, they have also selected his works three times as "Top-10 Romance Novel of the Year." NPR and B&N listed other works as "Best 5 of the Year."

As a 30-year project manager with a geophysics degree who has: designed and built houses, flown and jumped out of planes, and solo-sailed a 50' ketch. He is awed by what's possible. More at: www.mlbuchman.com.

Other works by M. L. Buchman: *(* - also in audio)*

Thrillers

Dead Chef
Swap Out!
One Chef!
Two Chef!

Miranda Chase
Drone*
Thunderbolt*

Romantic Suspense

Delta Force
Target Engaged*
Heart Strike*
Wild Justice*
Midnight Trust*

Firehawks
MAIN FLIGHT
Pure Heat
Full Blaze
Hot Point*
Flash of Fire*
Wild Fire
SMOKEJUMPERS
Wildfire at Dawn*
Wildfire at Larch Creek*
Wildfire on the Skagit*

The Night Stalkers
MAIN FLIGHT
The Night Is Mine
I Own the Dawn
Wait Until Dark
Take Over at Midnight
Light Up the Night
Bring On the Dusk
By Break of Day
AND THE NAVY
Christmas at Steel Beach
Christmas at Peleliu Cove

WHITE HOUSE HOLIDAY
Daniel's Christmas*
Frank's Independence Day*
Peter's Christmas*
Zachary's Christmas*
Roy's Independence Day*
Damien's Christmas*

5E
Target of the Heart
Target Lock on Love
Target of Mine
Target of One's Own

Shadow Force: Psi
At the Slightest Sound*
At the Quietest Word*

White House Protection Force
Off the Leash*
On Your Mark*
In the Weeds*

Contemporary Romance

Eagle Cove
Return to Eagle Cove
Recipe for Eagle Cove
Longing for Eagle Cove
Keepsake for Eagle Cove

Henderson's Ranch
Nathan's Big Sky*
Big Sky, Loyal Heart*
Big Sky Dog Whisperer*

Love Abroad
Heart of the Cotswolds: England
Path of Love: Cinque Terre, Italy

Other works by M. L. Buchman:

Contemporary Romance (cont)

Where Dreams
Where Dreams are Born
Where Dreams Reside
Where Dreams Are of Christmas
Where Dreams Unfold
Where Dreams Are Written

Science Fiction / Fantasy

Deities Anonymous
Cookbook from Hell: Reheated
Saviors 101

Single Titles
The Nara Reaction
Monk's Maze
the Me and Elsie Chronicles

Non-Fiction

Strategies for Success
Managing Your Inner Artist/Writer
Estate Planning for Authors*
Character Voice
Narrate and Record Your Own Audiobook*

Short Story Series by M. L. Buchman:

Romantic Suspense

Delta Force
Delta Force

Firehawks
The Firehawks Lookouts
The Firehawks Hotshots
The Firebirds

The Night Stalkers
The Night Stalkers
The Night Stalkers 5E
The Night Stalkers CSAR
The Night Stalkers Wedding Stories

US Coast Guard
US Coast Guard

White House Protection Force
White House Protection Force

Contemporary Romance

Eagle Cove
Eagle Cove

Henderson's Ranch
Henderson's Ranch

Where Dreams
Where Dreams

Thrillers

Dead Chef
Dead Chef

Science Fiction / Fantasy

Deities Anonymous
Deities Anonymous

Other
The Future Night Stalkers
Single Titles

Sign up for M. L. Buchman's
newsletter today

and receive:
Release News
Free Short Stories
a Free Book

Get your free book today. Do it now.
free-book.mlbuchman.com

www.ingramcontent.com/pod-product-compliance
Lightning Source LLC
Chambersburg PA
CBHW020140130526
44591CB00030B/167